MARCO  POLO

D1070261

NEW

YORK

CANADA   Maine

Michigan   New
            York
Wisconsin   New York
        Pennsylvania
Chicago   New Jersey
        Ohio   Washington
Illinois   D.C.
USA   Indiana
Missouri   Kentucky   Virginia
                    North
    Tennessee   Carolina
Arkansas   South
            Carolina   ATLANTIC
                        OCEAN
    Alabama
Mississippi   Georgia

Louisiana   Florida

    Gulf of   BAHAMAS
    Mexico   Miami

WITHDRAWN

www.marco-polo.com

GET MORE OUT OF YOUR MARCO POLO GUIDE

IT'S AS SIMPLE AS THIS

1 go.marco-polo.com/new

2 download and discover

GO!

WORKS OFFLINE!

6 **INSIDER TIPS**
Our top 15 Insider Tips

8 **BEST OF...**
- Great places for free
- Only in New York
- And if it rains?
- Relax and chill out

12 **INTRODUCTION**
Discover New York!

18 **WHAT'S HOT**
There are lots of new things to discover in New York

20 **IN A NUTSHELL**
Background information on New York

26 **SIGHTSEEING**
28 Lower Manhattan
34 Chinatown, Little Italy & Soho
37 Greenwich Village, East Village & Lower East Side
40 Midtown
48 Uptown & Central Park
55 Other districts
59 Further afield

60 **FOOD & DRINK**
Top culinary tips

72 **SHOPPING**
For a fun-filled shopping spree!

SYMBOLS

INSIDER TIP Insider Tip

★ Highlight

●●●● Best of ...

Scenic view

Responsible travel: for ecological or fair trade aspects

(*) Telephone numbers that are not toll-free

PRICE CATEGORIES HOTELS

Expensive	over 250$
Moderate	140–250$
Budget	under 140$

Prices for a double room per night including tax

PRICE CATEGORIES RESTAURANTS

Expensive	over $45
Moderate	$23–45
Budget	under $23

Prices based on an average meal of several courses without drinks and tip

On the cover: Meadows, wildflowers and skyscrapers p. 22 | Cocktails on cloud nine p. 84

CONTENTS

82 **ENTERTAINMENT**
Where to go?

96 **WHERE TO STAY**
From low budget
to luxury

106 **DISCOVERY TOURS**
106 New York at a glance
111 Strange worlds
114 Explore "new" Downtown
116 The best of the best
119 The beauty of Brooklyn

122 **TRAVEL WITH KIDS**
Best things to do with kids

124 **FESTIVALS & EVENTS**
All dates at a glance

126 **LINKS, BLOGS, APPS & MORE**
Plan ahead and use on the go

128 **TRAVEL TIPS**
From A to Z

136 **STREET ATLAS & INDEX**

166 **INDEX & CREDITS**

168 **DOS & DON'TS**

DID YOU KNOW?
Time to chill → p. 32
Giant wheel → p. 44
Fit in the city → p. 51
Spotlight on sports → p. 58
Favourite eateries → p. 64
Local specialities → p. 68
For TV series fans → p. 95
More than a good
night's sleep → p. 100
Currency converter → p. 131
For bookworms and
film buffs → p. 132
Weather → p. 135

MAPS IN THE GUIDEBOOK
(138 A1) Page numbers and
coordinates refer to the street
atlas and the general map of
New York
(0) Site/address located off
the map
Coordinates are also given for
places that are not marked
on the street atlas

(*A–B 2–3*) refers to the
removable pull-out map

(*a–b 2–3*) refers to the
inset of the removable pull-
out map

FRONT COVER:
The best Highlights

BACK COVER:
Subway map

The best MARCO POLO Insider Tips

Our top 15 Insider Tips

INSIDER TIP Humble beginnings
The life of newly arrived New Yorkers in the 19th century was anything but easy, as the faithfully reproduced *Tenement Museum* impressively shows (photo right) → p. 40

INSIDER TIP Film-making up close
Take a look behind the scenes at the *Museum of the Moving Image.* Not only learn how films are cut and sound recorded, but also create your own flip-book movie → p. 57

INSIDER TIP Club par excellence
Live concerts, dancing, karaoke, comedy and ping-pong are all on offer at *The Bell House,* one of the trendiest clubs in Brooklyn → p. 88

INSIDER TIP World affairs lunch
Yes, there's a *canteen* at the United Nations, too! You can rub shoulders with politicians while you have lunch at the UN Building in Midtown with a view of the East River → p. 68

INSIDER TIP Asian delight
Not a vegetarian menu: the hip *Momofuku Ssäm Bar* in East Village serves imaginative meat dishes → p. 66

INSIDER TIP A street vendor worth hunting down
Before you go out to eat you need to check Facebook, Twitter or the *Schnitzel & Things* website: to hunt down where this food truck will be parked – its location changes daily → p. 70

INSIDER TIP Vintage wonderland
Rummage through masses of dresses, trousers, jackets and shoes, classic and hip vintage wear, in one of the *Beacon's Closet* stores → p. 77

INSIDER TIP An unusual music workout
Ever heard of the shuffleboard? Give it a try to the sounds of DJ music and drinks at the bar at *Royal Palm Shuffle* → p. 87

INSIDER TIP **The pharmacist is "in"**
Green absinth is served by waiters dressed in white lab coats at *Apothéke* – the name fits, and this place in Chinatown seems more like a stage than a bar → p. 84

INSIDER TIP **Party beneath chandeliers**
Welcome to the home of the Polish community where rock and indie bands play the music of today in a 1950s ballroom – the *Warsaw Club* is a timeless gem → p. 91

INSIDER TIP **Off to the island**
A ferry runs from Manhattan to *Governors Island*, an adventure playground with lots of atmosphere, green meadows, festivals and events – almost all free of charge → p. 57

INSIDER TIP **Sea sensation**
The rooms in the historical *Jane Hotel* are called cabins and are decorated like berths on a ship. It has a marvellous view of the Hudson River → p. 100

INSIDER TIP **Flying high**
Learn to "fly" fearlessly with a safety net and no fear of landing. The *Trapeze School* in Hudson River Park is an opportunity to become a circus performer for the day as a juggler, trampolinist or trapeze artist → p. 123

INSIDER TIP **Ode to joy**
Not to be missed are the many *open air concerts* of the world renowned Metropolitan Opera held in various parks including a picnic. They are among the most impressive New York experiences to be had in the summer (for free) → p. 93

INSIDER TIP **Much more than just a park**
The *Brooklyn Bridge Park* is chock-full of fun: kayaks, beach volleyball, grills, live music, open-air movies, playgrounds, a beach, a historic carousel and much, much more (photo left) → p. 57

BEST OF...

FOR FREE

● *Visit a museum of superlatives*
A shrine to 20th- and 21st-century art – and all for free? On Friday afternoons there is no admission charge for the extraordinary collections of *MoMA*. Don't miss it! (photo) → **p. 43**

● *The ferry not to be missed*
When the *Staten Island Ferry* pulls away from the shore you get to see the full sweep of the Manhattan skyline from the Statue of Liberty and Ellis Island across to New Jersey on the one side and Brooklyn on the other. This free trip is full of magic! → **p. 33**

● *Native Americans in the heart of the big city*
What the Wild West was really like: the *National Museum of the American Indian* shows how much Hollywood has shaped our view of the Indians. Admission to the world of the Native Americans in an imposing building in the south of Manhattan is free → **p. 32**

● *City tour with local guides*
Big Apple Greeters are a group of engaged New Yorkers who take pleasure in showing visitors around their hometown. A good way to make new friends – and all you have to pay is a smile → **p. 36**

● *Gospel songs that strike a chord*
The devotion of the congregation at a *gospel church service* in Harlem – clad in their Sunday best with flamboyant hats – is guaranteed to give you goose pimples! → **p. 52**

● *Mini stage with maxi music*
The small, but first-rate club *Barbes* brings excellent music to the stage, free of charge, with a mix of jazz, world beats and East European tunes → **p. 88**

● *Reveal the mysteries of brewing*
What actually happens in the copper vats in which beer ferments? It doesn't even cost a cent to discover the secrets of making beer on the *Brooklyn Brewery Tour* → **p. 70**

●●●● Dots in guidebook refer to "Best of..." tips

ONLY IN NEW YORK
Unique experiences

● *Reflections on the 9/11 site*
The poignant *9/11 Memorial* is a place for contempla-
tion. Three waterfalls tumble into two huge pools
that mark the exact spots where the twin towers used to be → **p. 29**

● *Pedestrian zone in a sea of lights*
With parts of *Times Square* on 42nd Street
having been declared a pedestrian precinct, visitors can now take in the world-
famous neon lights from the comfort of a
chair or seated on one of the steps → **p. 26**

● *Department store of superlatives*
Macy's is the biggest department store and a
New York institution. Its parade on July 4th is an
extravagant spectacle with gigantic balloons and
dancing cheerleaders → **p. 76**

● *A bird's-eye view of the Big Apple*
Gaze over the length of Central Park and the Manhattan skyline from
the *Roof Garden* of the Metropolitan Museum. While the people below
run around like busy bees, you can sit back and enjoy the view with a
cocktail in hand → **p. 54**

● *Tempting delicacies*
SoHo is known for its large lofts belonging to stars like Madonna, its
superb galleries and boutiques and its gourmet grocery stores. The
most famous is *Dean & DeLuca* which has been importing delicacies
from around the world for more than 30 years – delicious but pricey!
→ **p. 75**

● *A breath of fresh air*
Rambling *Central Park* with its trees, boulders and waterfalls was
established more than a century ago. Today this green belt is a roller-
bladers', joggers', nannies' and dog-lovers' paradise. Laze on the lawns,
row on the lakes or listen to a concert – there is plenty to do here
(photo) → **p. 50**

● *Donut delight*
The *Doughnut Plant* steps it up a notch when it comes to the stereo-
typical donut. Their decadent donuts come in a selection of unusual
flavours (like pistachio, peanut butter or blueberry) and shapes → **p. 62**

ONLY IN

BEST OF...

● *Egyptian temples, American paintings*
You could easily spend a whole week in the *Metropolitan Museum of Art.* The remarkable collection is one of the finest in the world → p. 53

● *Parlor jazz in Harlem*
Marjorie Eliot and her *Parlor Entertainment:* live jazz entertains guests from around the world while waxing lyrical about Martin Luther King and civil rights. An excellent afternoon's entertainment! → p. 92

● *Haven for book lovers*
Rummage through the huge array of books at the *Strand Book Store.* It's just as easy to find current bestsellers as rare art editions here → p. 75

● *Himalayan art*
Mandalas and meditation images transport visitors to the highest mountains of the world at the *Rubin Museum.* The elegantly designed building also houses a restaurant, a bar and a museum shop → p. 39

● *Shopping and eating in an old factory*
Feel like a brownie straight from the oven or a fresh lobster at Lobster Place? The *Chelsea Market* awaits with the industrial charm of a renovated factory and its gourmet delights (photo) → p. 75

● *Fitness by the river*
Chelsea Piers is a massive sports and entertainment complex on the Hudson River in Chelsea. Dancing, bowling, basketball, climbing, swimming and golf are some of the activities on offer → p. 51

● *A relaxing coffee break*
The lattes and baked treats behind the large windows of *Amy's Bread* are excellent. Greenwich Village with its cobblestone streets and old houses is quite charming in any weather → p. 62

RAIN

RELAX AND CHILL OUT
Take it easy and spoil yourself

● *New energy for tired limbs*
In *Chinatown* there is a masseuse on every corner, just what you need to ease your stiff shoulders and tired feet. There is a lot to be said for the 2000-year-old Chinese therapies on offer → p. 32

● *Water under the bridge*
Relax and let yourself be gently rocked as you float to the strains of the classical music on the *Bargemusic*, an old barge docked beneath Brooklyn Bridge with a spectacular view of the Manhattan skyline → p. 93

● *Manhattan sights by boat*
The *Circle Line* boat takes you around the island. The relaxing three hour tour is full of interesting facts and stories and is an excellent way to familiarise yourself with Uptown, Downtown, Eastside and Westside → p. 128

● *Garden on railway tracks*
The elevated *High Line Park* is not only a landscape of greenery and plants. You can also stretch out on one of the wooden loungers and watch cruise ships, ferries and sailing boats go by → p. 22

● *A quiet corner*
Hidden away on a side street in SoHo, the *Housing Works Bookstore Cafe* is a relaxing oasis amidst the hectic of Manhattan. You can browse away to your heart's content in peace and quiet → p. 76

● *Balance and harmony Asian-style*
Seated Indian-style on cushions, visitors to the *Shambhala Meditation Center* are taught meditation and total relaxation in the traditional Asian way → p. 32

● *Cocktails under the stars*
Sip a cocktail at sunset and enjoy the views across the city from the rooftop bar *Press Lounge*. Its glistening swimming pool and views are the best backdrop for looking back on your day (photo) → p. 87

INTRODUCTION

DISCOVER NEW YORK!

New York City is synonymous with the American dream and the only way to understand this massive, adrenaline-fuelled, influential and nerve-racking metropolis is to come and see it for yourself. Wake up to the sounds of the city that never sleeps – cars hooting, sirens howling and screeching brakes. The *New York feeling* is something you have to experience up close.

New York is many things, among them a vibrant global capital of commerce – hectic, loud, provocative, immense and powerful. Dedicated in 2014 and opened to the public in May 2015, *One World Trade Center* (1WTC) dominates the southern Manhattan skyline. At a height of 541 m/1,776 ft, it is meant to symbolize the renaissance of Downtown Manhattan. New York has also retained its title as the *world's entertainment capital*: Every evening it plays host to a diverse array of film premiers, musicals, ballets, gala theatre events, rock and pop concerts, jazz sessions and high-end opera, plus its multitude of cutting-edge clubs perfectly encapsulate the current zeitgeist. The audiences are varied, enthusiastic, discerning and above all, critical. If you can make it here, you can make it anywhere, as Frank Sinatra says in his famous hit "New York, New York".

Photo: Downtown Manhattan with One World Trade Center

In *Downtown Manhattan* (in other words everything south of 14th Street), the restaurant and bar scene here is far more exciting than in Midtown or in northern Manhattan. Trendy new hotels, hip nightclubs and daring architecture such as the Cooper Union building, the New Museum and the Trade Center Station (opened in 2015) draw locals and tourists alike to the south of the city. Here the visitor will find old run-down buildings next to stylish bars, the historical next to the modern and it is these contrasts that lure the visitor. Every year in May international filmmakers and Hollywood movie stars descend on the city to attend the TriBeCa Film Festival that was founded by Robert de Niro. The event is a magnet for movie buffs, celebrity hunters and everyone who is fan of the glitz and glamour of red carpet events.

> ## Historic buildings accompanied by modern glamour

As night descends, Manhattan feels as if it is one single, massive party. In their major hit "Empire State of Mind", Jay Z and Alicia Keys sang an ode to the glittering concrete jungle of New York and its powers of attraction. The song became the new hymn of this city of success and opportunity. But, the New Yorkers have also become more contemplative. The protest movement *Occupy Wall Street* has prompted much discussion and the revelations of the whistle-blower Edward Snowden shook up the way many residents think about the world.

As the *media hub of the United States*, everything cultural this city has to offer tends to be amplified. Key global television broadcasters, major news magazines and the *New York Times* – arguably the world's most important daily newspaper – are all based here. All the leading publishing houses are based in the city where they keep their eye set on the global market. The city attracts creative people like no other: actors, artists, authors, designers as well as advertisers and software developers. For centuries New York has thrived on, and drawn its energy from, the constantly changing cycle of boom and bust.

Today around *8.5 million people* live the city. Once the world's largest, it can no longer lay claim to that title as it has been overtaken by other megacities. Metropolitan New York also includes areas such as Long Island, Westchester County, New Jersey and Connecticut and has 24 million inhabitants, and most work in Manhattan, the city centre. Added to this figure are all the tourists who join the throng on the fast paced sidewalks.

After World War II the *United Nations* set up its headquarters in New York. After the shocking *events of 9/11*, New York became a political focal point for American politics and the UN headquarters have been in the international spotlight for years, especially because of the wars in the Middle East. But the heart of New York doesn't beat for politics. Washington, D.C. remains the real political heart of America.

Mayor Michael Bloomberg spearheaded a drive to turn New York into an *environmentally friendly city*. *Times Square* is now a pedestrian precinct, and there are new cycle paths everywhere (700 km/435 miles in length). His successor since 2014, the liberal Bill de Blasio, has continued to push the green revolution forward on the busy streets of Manhattan. Traffic islands have been turned into little oases with bistro tables, chairs and umbrellas while a former elevated railway track has been outfitted with wooden lounge chairs.

The green revolution is still on the move

The lengths of Manhattan Island along the Hudson River are now parkland and beneath Brooklyn Bridge miles of river frontage have been reclaimed and boast an urban beach, boat trips and playgrounds. Even the *Empire State Building* has undergone extensive renovations to optimise its energy consumption. New bus lanes have made it faster to navigate the congested streets in an environmentally-friendly way.

The Guggenheim Museum is a unique building, both inside and out

The ringing bells of the bicycle rickshaws herald a quick, safe and truly green way to get from place to place. Or you can hop on a bike yourself thanks in part to the large-scale Citi-Bike programme. However, at times it is still easiest to get around on foot.

New York has for some time now prided itself on being one of America's most *pedestrian-friendly cities*. The grid layout and numerical street numbers are easy to follow; many of the city's attractions are located in close proximity to one another and so you should find your way around with ease. Whereas in the 1980s, it wasn't difficult to land unexpectedly in a rather seedy part of town, nowadays the danger of drifting astray in New York is no greater than in any other major city. Nonetheless, it still pays to keep your eyes open.

New York is a city of contrasts. Winters are dry with freezing temperatures. In summer the mercury can easily rise into the 80s (over 30 degrees Celsius) and it can be very, very humid. The endless grey concrete jungle juxtaposes with the expansive green belt of *Central Park*. *Skyscrapers* dwarf church spires. There is a constant dichotomy between large and small, rich and poor, old and new. Every race and nation is represented here. Driven by the hope of a better future, many have turned their backs on their countries of origin for political or economic reasons. All have brought with them a touch of home, be it cuisine from Ethiopia, samba dancing from Brazil, festive parades from Italy or the dragon dance from China all contributing to making this a city of unimaginable diversity.

Driven by the hope of a better future

The mix of immigrant populations in New York is constantly in flux, In the 19th century, immigrants from Ireland, Germany, Austria and Russian changed the rather English character of the city. At the beginning of the 20th century Italian and Polish immigrants joined them and New York later became a safe haven for the persecuted Jews of Europe. This *melting pot* or fusion of diverse cultures is unique to New York and is unrivalled in the United States. It is for this reason that New Yorkers also consider themselves as a distinct breed, culturally aware, abreast of the economic situation, enquiring, tolerant and arrogant at times. But this description only really seems to apply to the white New Yorkers who dominate the city although they make up less than 50 percent of the actual population. In more recent years, the waves of immigrants have included millions of people from central and South America, hundreds of thousands of Chinese, Koreans and Vietnamese, as well as many African Americans from the southern states.

The recent influx has been so great that the city has almost lost one of its most important attributes: the ease with which it is able to merge, mix and integrate many diverse cultures. This has completely *changed its character*. In 1989 the first African American mayor of New York, David Dinkins, described it best in his acceptance speech when he said, "New York is not a melting pot anymore. It is a gorgeous mosaic of people".

9/11 Memorial – a dignified monument to a horrible tragedy

Sadly the "gorgeous mosaic" symbolising equality is cracking. The immigrants are invariably poor and often illegal while those working on Wall Street have seen their salaries skyrocket to dizzying heights once again after the financial crisis. Although some brokers may have lost their jobs, those remaining have once again been able to make huge profits in a short space of time.

New York's flaws are discernible if you simply examine its five *boroughs*. Independently they could each be an entire city. This was indeed the case up until 1898 before Greater New York was formed by merging Manhattan, Brooklyn, Queens, Staten Island and the Bronx. Today *Brooklyn* is gaining in popularity thanks to its museums, architecture, massive Prospect Park, designer boutiques and sophisticated restaurants. Williamsburg in northern Brooklyn has become the perfect *quarter for a night out* on the town. Here young artists and designers have created a network of galleries, restaurants and interesting small shops that make it worthwile to visit this

Between Harlem and the Statue of Liberty

area. This creative buzz is snow spreading east – into the *Bushwick* area. But tourists usually make Manhattan – between the Statue of Liberty and Harlem – their ultimate destination. After all, it is the heart of the city!

WHAT'S HOT

1 Flowers and more

Multifunctional Flower pots are on display in the shop windows, behind them is the bar: *Sycamore Flower Shop & Bar (1118 Cortelyou Road | www.sycamorebrooklyn.com)* (photo) is a trendy watering hole in Brooklyn. During the day it sells arty flowers, at night it serves tasty snacks and good cocktails. Florist *Zezé (938 1st Av.)* is just as multifunctional selling flowers, furniture and home décor. At *Flower Girl (245 Eldridge Street | flowergirlnyc.com)* small gifts and elegant flower arrangements are sold.

A good read

2

Reading journeys Small, often specialized book-stores flourish in the city. A mix of books with a café can be found, for example, in SoHo at *McNally Jackson (52 Prince Street | www.mcnallyjackson.com)* (photo). The finest photography books are also shelved in NoHo at *Dashwood Books (33 BondStreet | www.dashwood books.com).* In Brooklyn, *Greenlight Bookstore (686 Ful-ton Street | www.greenlightbookstore.com)* offers a fine selection of books plus interesting readings with wine and small talk. *Kitchen Arts & Letters (1435 Lexington Av. | kitchenartsandletters.com)* on Upper East Side sells nothing but cookery books.

3 Urban jungle

Green Apple The city's parks are opening their doors to campers. Guided excursions with park rangers have transformed the *New York State Parks (www.nycgov parks.org)* into adventure parks for adults and children. After an interesting and entertaining tour, you get to camp in one of the parks over-night. There are canoe trips for those into ad-venture sport, also lectures on herbal medicine and survival skills.

There are lots of new things to discover in New York. A few of the most interesting are listed below

Water, wind and waves

Boat tours New York travels by boat – or, to be more exact, by ferry. To make better use of the waterways, New York's mayor Bill de Blasio wants to link Manhattan and the other five boroughs with new ferry lines. To avoid congested streets and crowded subway cars, New Yorkers already take boats, for example from Manhattan (e.g. from 35th Street on the East River), Dumbo, Williamsburg, Greenpoint and Queens. In summer *Seastreak (www.seastreak.com)* chugs to Sandy Hook for sunbathing on the beach in New Jersey in only 35 minutes. From 2017 various routes on the *Hudson (www.nywaterway.com)* and the *East River (www.eastriverferry.com)* will be added, for example to the south of Brooklyn and trendy Rockaways in Queens.

Queens is king!

Cool and authentic For a long time Manhattan and Brooklyn were its cooler sisters, but Queens is getting its act together, and has the most colourful (and largest) population in New York. The boutique hotels are cheaper, the restaurants more relaxed, and there is also plenty of art to see in western Queens in Long Island City, for example in the *sculpture park (www.socrates sculpturepark.org, photo)*, the *Noguchi Museum (www.noguchi.org)*, the *Fisher Landau Center for Art (www.flcart.org)* and in *MoMA PS1 (www.momaps1.org)*. Further east in Queens lies Flushing, New York's biggest Chinatown, with authentic Asian food on every corner. If you want to get away from the crowds, go to Far Rockaway, the surfing paradise in Queens, and take to the waves.

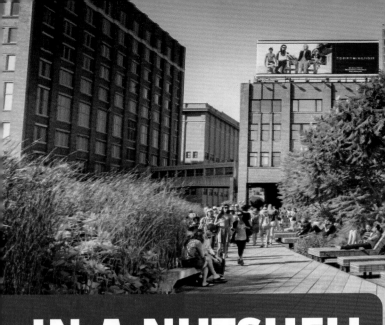

IN A NUTSHELL

THE BIG APPLE

The expression has its beginnings in the jazz scene before World War II. If your performance made it to New York you were getting a bite from the Big Apple. Not only were musicians' earnings in New York much better but the city also held the promise of a career stepping stone.

COOL HERITAGE

Harlem is full of energy. Its music, art and restaurant scenes are buzzing. To come here is to be immersed in a many-sided history: At the beginning of the 20th century, numerous blacks from the South migrated north to New York. Among them were artists ranging from the writer Langsten Hughes to the lat-

er world-famous musicians Duke Ellington and Louis Armstrong. This culture legacy can still be felt in Harlem and the Bronx, the birthplace of Hip Hop in the 1970s, at places like the *Apollo Theater (see p. 95)*, the *Studio Museum in Harlem (144 W 125th Street | www. studiomuseum.org)* and Jazz clubs including *Showmans Jazz Club (375 W 125th Street | tel. 1 212 8 64 89 41 | www. showmansjazzclub.com)*.

The art scene in the south Bronx is served by the *Bronx Culture Trolley (Oct–Dec, Feb–Aug first Wed in month, free entrance | www.bronxarts.org)*. This streetcar stops at cultural sites, restaurants or event locations. It is also worth checking out the film screenings at the *Bronx Documentary Center (www.bronx*

Skyscrapers, island hopping, musicals and this unique atmosphere – the Big Apple has its own attitude to life

doc.org) and the photo exhibitions at the *Bronx Museum of the Arts*.

DIZZYING HEIGHTS

If you suffer from vertigo, New York is a good place to overcome it. After all, the tallest skyscrapers in the city were usually also the world's tallest at the same time. This still holds true: One World Trade Center is 541 m/1,775 ft tall, higher than any other building in the western world. It is meant to show that terrorism cannot triumph over freedom. It replaces the twin towers of the World Trade Center that collapsed on 11 September 2001, when terrorists crashed two passenger aircraft into them. When they were completed in 1971 and 1973, the twin towers were in line with the New York tradition: a world record at 419.7 m/1,377 ft. The first skyscrapers were built in the late 19th century. From the Chrysler Building (1930, 319 m/1,047 ft) to the Empire State Building (443 m/1,421 ft to the tip of the lightning rod), opened in 1931, there was a period of monumental construction. The shortage of building land alone is not an adequate explanation for the enthusiasm – it is also a form of self-reassurance, and a demonstration of power and confidence. The art-deco style, brilliantly executed in the Chrysler Building, gave way to the modernism of Ludwig Mies van der Rohe (Lever House and Seagram Building). Glass, simplicity and functional quality replaced the adornments.

The new architecture of the city is by no means modest: The impressive Cooper Union University building, opened in 2009, is a structure with a vertical section that looks like a massive tear. Next to the Brooklyn Bridge and completed in 2011 is the Beekman Tower by Frank Gehry, an apartment block with 76 floors. The remarkable and stylish building has a façade of stainless steel that reflects light and gives the illusion that it ripples and undulates. The Beekman Tower first had to cede its title as the highest residential building in the city to the skyscraper One57 in Midtown (306 m/1,003 ft) and just a few months later to 432 Park Avenue. Opened in 2015, this latter building tops out at a height of 396 m/1,300 ft and will be surpassed in 2018 by the Central Park Tower, at 472 m/1,549 ft.

D ESIREABLE DOORMEN

Uniformed doormen are part and parcel of elite areas like the Upper East and Upper West Side. There are 100,000 or more of them in New York and they are the status symbols of the wealthy elite. A world where people have spacious, luxury homes in huge apartment blocks and have a doorman at their beck and call. The doormen assist residents by holding open doors, carrying shopping parcels, signing in couriered items, flagging down cabs as well as by screening and announcing visitors. Being a doorman is a well-paid and sought after job.

D OWNTOWN

Downtown is the southern half of Manhattan and is synonymous with young up-and-coming and creative New Yorkers. In contrast, Uptown is the northern part west and east of Central Park which has immaculate and glamorous apartments with their own libraries, servants' rooms, large dining halls, thick walls, high ceilings and fireplaces all of which shape the image of the chic lifestyle its residents enjoy. The image of Uptown residents is conservative. They are considered part of the establishment, which means anyone wanting to be seen as being part of the creative, hip and in-crowd will want to have an address in TriBeCa or the East and West Village.

G OING GREEN

For parsnips, apple pie or juicy organic fruit – New Yorkers love their *farmers' markets*. More than 60 weekend markets are held across the city. The successful health food chains *Trader Joe's* and *Whole Foods* even polish their fruit before presenting it in even rows in their large stores. Traffic-calming measures and new bike paths are appearing on New York's streets and squares. In the city's 1,700 (!) public parks you can make a truly leisurely exploration of New York on a bike, with an organic picnic in the basket. ★ ● *High Line* (146 B–C 1–3) (*D B–C 9–11*) (*www.thehighline.org*) in Chelsea even has wild flowers growing on it and it has become symbolic for an environmentally friendly New York.

In Manhattan, traffic-calming measures are being introduced to the streets, *Times Square* is already a pedestrian precinct. *Hudson River Park* on Manhattan's west side makes an excellent urban retreat with its lawns, tennis courts and paddle-boats as well as the *Brooklyn Bridge Park* on the East River.

ISLAND HOPPING

New York City is made up of a whole series of islands – a fact that is easy to forget. Manhattan itself is one, the Statue of Liberty stands tall on *Liberty Island* and *Ellis Island* is where arriving immigrants were received until 1954. The city's shore is 577 miles long. A ferry will take you from the southernmost tip of Manhattan across to *Governors Island* for a picnic on its lawns, with crazy golf, hammocks and tree houses, art exhibitions and concerts. The ferry to *Staten Island,* like Manhattan one of the Five Boroughs, is

invariably accompanied by people on kayaks and at the Brooklyn, Queens and Manhattan water taxi stations you will see commuters, on their way to work or out shopping, embarking and disembarking from the bright yellow taxi boats.

Swinging high up on the east end of 60th Street is the ✴ aerial tramway that takes you to *Roosevelt Island* in East River. Don't fail to go to the Franklin D. Roosevelt Four Freedom Park at the south tip: on the right is Manhattan, on the left Brooklyn – a fantastic view! *Randall Island* can be reached on foot via the bridge on 103rd Street and the subway and bus will take you to *City Island* which is a sailor's paradise. The newly renovated *Coney Island* in the south of Brooklyn is once again attracting many visitors. Amuse-

Nostalgic and quite crazy: Luna Park on Coney Island

ment parks and rollercoasters, the beach and an aquarium and the prospect of a Russian meal all draw visitors to this seaside peninsula. People from around the world come here to enjoy a stroll along the wide promenade and to enjoy New York island life.

ON STAGE!

Musicals have always been closely associated with New York, but now they are surrounded by new hype – "only" because of a single super-hit, the hip-hop musical "Hamilton" about one of the founding fathers of the USA. The songs are sung on every corner, and a ticket on the black market costs a cool $1,500. Broadway has rarely been so exciting! Year on year, 13 million spectators come to the shows, even though they have to pay steep prices for tickets.

The risk of producing a new musical or theatre production on Broadway is huge. Not only have the costs of development and advertising risen – the expectations of audiences, spoiled by movies, are also higher. Treats such as the musical "The Book of Mormon", a biting satire filled with wit, imagination and songs that get under your skin, and "Fun Home" about a lesbian couple in a undertaker's business are worth every dollar, however – an authentic musical experience!

It is worth taking a chance and seeing an Off-Off-Broadway piece. With smaller budgets and less glitz and glamour they tend to be more imaginative and provocative. Incidentally a theatre's proximity to the famous avenue has absolutely nothing to do with it being classed Broadway, Off-Broadway or Off-Off-Broadway. It is an on Broadway theatre if it has more than 500 seats; if it has 100 seats it is an Off-Broadway theatre and any theatre with fewer seats is Off-Off-Broadway.

PRICEY NEIGHBOURHOODS

New York's residents are often on the run, not from the IRS or the law, but from rising rentals, the loud music of new neighbours or from the bars and clubs that never sleep. This has always been the case: *Greenwich Village* used to be busy with the coming and going of authors and artists but its narrow streets and quaint houses were turned into lucrative rental cash cows. The creative minds and free spirits have now had to make way for the movers and shakers. In *Little Italy* you will find very few genuine Italian-Americans anymore. *Chinatown* is the culprit: With its cheap labour and great variety of shops and restaurants it is bursting at the seams, spreading northwards and slowly encroaching on the Italian quarter.

The *Lower East Side* has historically always been a working-class neighbourhood. Jewish families from Eastern Europe came here to start their American dream. Here too, gentrification arrived some time ago. Today the district is a haven of designer boutiques, high-end restaurants, trendy bars and small art galleries.

In the hip district of *Williamsburg* prices of loft apartments are skyrocketing. Its young residents are being forced to look to other parts of Brooklyn for alternatives. Especially *Greenpoint* and *Bushwick* are benefiting from the influx of ambitious young people.

For some, the nightlife in Manhattan is too boring, so they head east to Williamsburg and Bushwick in Brooklyn to party and dance the nights away. These districts are known for their music scenes. The clubs are often housed in former factory buildings or warehouses, bearing names such as *Output, Verboten, Bossa Nova Civic Club* and *TBA Brooklyn*. The prices are lower, the music is cooler and there are quite unique places such as *Bizarre Bar* where strange, circus-like performances are staged.

ROOFTOP BARS

See the city from above: bars on high-rise rooftops and terraces have gorgeous views of skyscrapers, urban canyons and a sea of lights at night. Manhattan is densely populated, the pace of life hectic and its visitors discerning. Necessity is the mother of invention and today a skyscrapers' architecture will invariably incorporate a roof terrace. Many hotels offer their guests the option of enjoying a lofty cocktail in their rooftop bars. The most impressive of these are the *Salon de Ning* at the Peninsula Hotel, *Press Lounge* at Ink48, *Le Bain* at The Standard Hotel, *230 Fifth* on Fifth Avenue and the lounge atop the Po39 hotel.

SUMMERTIME

In the summer months it is hot and humid in the city, and many New Yorkers choose to leave for the country. East of the metropolis lies *Long Island* with its legendary villages and hamlets know as the Hamptons with its very inviting 62-mile stretch of fine sandy beaches as well as Fire Island off the coast. These Atlantic beaches were once the domain of whalers and smugglers but are now where the East Coast in-crowd and Hollywood big names spend their summers feasting on lobsters and scallops.

Long Island is in the shape of a crocodile with its jaw open. The *Hamptons* are located in its lower "jaw". These picture-perfect old villages lie one after another along the coast like a string of pearls: South Hampton, Bridgehampton, East Hampton and Amagansett. Montauk with its lighthouse forms the most eastern point. Charming villages with whitewashed, clapboard and wooden houses, narrow streets, small boutiques and cafés

all lend character to this exclusive and very pricey area.

The narrow barrier sandbar of *Fire Island* is located at Long Island's southernmost point. You take a boat across and once there you have to get about on foot. There are no cars and bicycles are restricted so you have to carry daypacks for your food, towels and reading material. Wooden walkways are leading to the beach. With conservation high on the agenda the is-

The endangered idyllic country retreat in the city – Williamsburg

land is full of deer and perfect for bird watching. The beaches of New Jersey are a cheaper destination. A train from Penn Station takes 1.5 hours to Asbury Park: swimming and surfing, yeah!

SIGHTSEEING

WHERE TO START?
Empire State Building (147 E2) *(Ⓜ E9)*: The eye-catching Empire State Building in art-deco style is the perfect launching pad. Whizz up to the top and enjoy sweeping views of the city.
Fifth Avenue is leading north to the major museums and Central Park and in the south Broadway is only a block away.
If you watch the sun set here on your first evening in New York, you will never forget the sight.
Subway: 34 Street-Herald Square, B, D, F, M, N, Q, R.

Faced with an enormous variety of options, at first glance the city may seem overwhelming. What to do first and what are the absolute must-sees?

New York City is full of bold and daring architecture concentrated in a relatively small area. Imposing skyscrapers, expansive bridges and statuesque churches make up its rich tapestry. And, in the middle of it all, there is a park just over a third of the size of London's Richmond Park. The best way to get around is on foot or on the subway. Outside Grand Central shoeshiners await customers who want gleaming footwear, but walk past them and go to ● ◐ *Times Square* and experience firsthand this iconic hub with its massive flashing billboards and adver-

The Empire State Building, SoHo, Staten Island Ferry, Central Park and Broadway – the constant hustle and bustle of the city that never sleeps

tisements. Car horns and squealing taxis have not disappeared, but there are tables and chairs too. Sit down and relax – and watch this astonishing, vibrant hub of Manhattan Island. Welcome to New York! A trip all round Manhattan by boat is a relaxing and informative tour, a helicopter ride more exciting, but also more expensive. Depending on your budget the rides last anything from six to 20 minutes.

New York has excellent museums. Find out which exhibitions are all the rage and which ones are worth visiting by checking the *New York Times (Fri and Sat),* the weekly magazines *New York Magazine, Time Out* and *The New Yorker* or the website *dks.thing.net.* Many museums offer audio tours that you can hire at the entrance to guide you through the exhibition for a small fee. Some museums do not charge a set admission but expect a

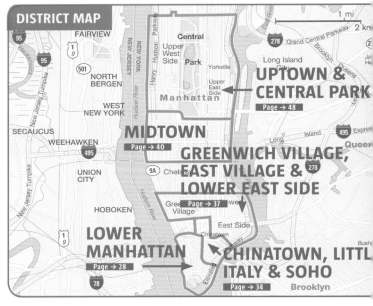

DISTRICT MAP

FAIRVIEW

NORTH BERGEN

WEST NEW YORK

SECAUCUS

WEEHAWKEN

UNION CITY

HOBOKEN

NEW JERSEY

Central
Upper West Side
Park

Manhattan

Yorkville

Upper East Side

UPTOWN & CENTRAL PARK
Page → 48

MIDTOWN
Page → 40

GREENWICH VILLAGE, EAST VILLAGE & LOWER EAST SIDE
Page → 37

LOWER MANHATTAN
Page → 28

Chelsea

Greenwich Village

East Side

Chinatown

CHINATOWN, LITTL ITALY & SOHO
Page → 34

Long Island City

Queens

Brooklyn

1 mi
2 km

The map shows the location of the most interesting districts. There is a detailed map of each district on which each of the sights described is numbered.

small donation. Americans in a position to do so are generally keen to pay, but donating what you can afford is not frowned upon. Plan ahead and buy your tickets for the Empire State Building, the Statue of Liberty and the Museum of Modern Art online. This will save you a lot of time that would be wasted in queues.

LOWER MANHATTAN

Versatile and interesting – Lower Manhattan has it all, from stylish restaurants to historical sites and impressive skyscrapers.

It is home to New York's world famous financial centre – Wall Street. This is also where the two towers of the Word Trade Center stood before 9/11, where the new One World Trade Center now stands and where the immigrants arrived – right up until the middle of the last century – to seek their fortune in the new world. Take a long walk around the gigantic buildings and along the narrow cobbled streets at the southernmost tip of Manhattan. For an impressive view of the southern Manhattan skyline from the water take a ferry ride out to Staten Island. Walk along the Hudson River through Battery Park to reach TriBeCa, where pricey restaurants are very popular with celebrities.

■1 9/11 MEMORIAL ⭐ ●
(142 B4) (*A16*)

On 11 September 2001, the World Trade Center was razed to the ground when hijacked passenger aircraft crashed into the twin towers. Ground Zero is now the site of an impressive monument to the terrorist attack: on the place where they stood from 1973, water falls on all sides into deep pools round whose edges the names of all the victims are engraved – a sight that makes a lasting impression on visitors. There is also an adjacent *Museum (Sun–Thu 9am–8pm, Fri–Sat 9am–9pm | admission $24, free on Tue after 5pm). Daily 7:30am–9pm | 120 Liberty Street | free admission | www.911memorial.org | subway: A, C, J, 2, 3, 4, 5 Fulton Street.*

Firemen, survivors, relatives of the victims and residents give tours. The *Tribute WTC Visitor Center (Mon–Sat 10am–6pm, Sun 10am–5pm | 120 Liberty Street | admission $25 | tours: Sun–Thu hourly 11am–3pm, Fri/Sat hourly 10:30am–3pm | costs $20 | www.tributewtc.org | subway: A, C, E Chambers Street)* also provides extensive information about 9/11 and its aftermath.

■2 BROOKFIELD PLACE
(142 A3–4) (*A16*)

The former World Trade Center on the southernmost tip of Manhattan across from Wall Street comprises office blocks, shops, apartments *(Battery Park City)*, yacht harbour and green areas. The *Winter Garden*, an atrium with a glass roof, has a variety of restaurants and shops, not to mention INSIDERTIP free concerts and exhibitions. *Information: "Events" section of www.brookfieldplaceny.com | West Street/between Vesey and Liberty Street | subway: A, C, J, M, Z, 1, 2, 3 Chambers Street*

⭐ **Brooklyn Bridge**
Enjoy the view of the Manhattan skyline when crossing the "eighth wonder of the world" → p. 30

⭐ **9/11 Memorial**
A poignant monument – waterfalls commemorate the terrorist attacks → p. 29

⭐ **Staten Island Ferry**
The perfect view of the Manhattan skyline – all for free → p. 33

⭐ **Statue of Liberty**
Iconic landmark → p. 33

⭐ **Fifth Avenue**
Shopping and strolling about → p. 38

⭐ **One World Trade Center**
An impressive solitary tower as a replacement for the Twin Towers → p. 32

⭐ **Empire State Building**
Well worth the wait: panoramic views from its 86th-floor viewing platform → p. 41

⭐ **Museum of Modern Art**
Art at the best museum in the world → p. 43

⭐ **Rockefeller Center**
A city within a city → p. 45

⭐ **American Museum of Natural History**
Dinosaurs and a journey into space → p. 50

⭐ **Central Park**
A green oasis in the midst of the concrete jungle → p. 50

⭐ **Guggenheim Museum**
Modern art in Frank Lloyd Wright's architectural masterpiece → p. 52

MARCO POLO HIGHLIGHTS

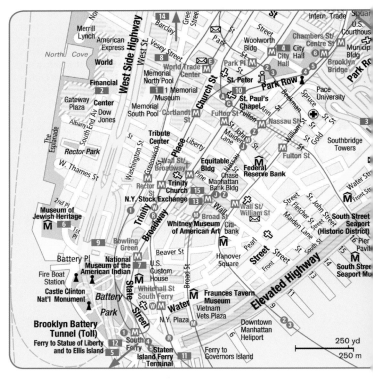

SIGHTSEEING IN LOWER MANHATTAN

1 9/11 Memorial
2 Brookfield Place
3 Brooklyn Bridge
4 City Hall
5 Ellis Island
6 Museum of Jewish Heritage
7 National Museum of the American Indian
8 One World Trade Center
9 The Skyscraper Museum
10 St Paul's Chapel
11 Staten Island Ferry
12 Statue of Liberty
13 Stock Exchange
14 TriBeCa
15 Wall Street

  pedestrian precinct

3 BROOKLYN BRIDGE ★
(143 D5) (⌖ D17)

The first bridge to connect Manhattan with Brooklyn was completed in 1883 after 13 years of construction by engineers John A. Roebling and son. Its two pylons, standing nearly 292 feet high, support hundreds of steel cables. The structure spans just over 1,738 feet above the East River and has been lauded as the eighth wonder of the world. The centre walkway that runs under its neo-Gothic arches gives you a stunning view of the Manhattan skyline. It is most striking when you INSIDER TIP walk towards Manhattan. To do so, take subway line A or C to High Street Station in Brooklyn or set out from Manhattan starting from Park Row/Centre Street *(subway: 4–6 Brooklyn Bridge/City Hall).*

▣4 CITY HALL (142 C3–4) *(𝄞 B16)*

Originally, the southern façade of the mayor's office (completed in 1812) was covered in marble but the northern façade in brick. At the time, the city fathers assumed that New York would not expand further north. If you want to tie the knot, go to the *Municipal Building* in Center Street and pay $35 by credit card for a marriage license *(Mon–Fri 8:30am–3:45pm | 141 Worth Street | www.cityclerk.nyc.gov). Broadway/ corner of Park Row street | subway: 6, N, Q, J, Z Canal Street*

▣5 ELLIS ISLAND (159 E6) *(𝄞 a–b 19–20)*

See how you feel in the role of a new immigrant to the USA: Around 12 million immigrants first stepped onto American soil at this transit centre. It all happened on this small island in New York Bay over a period of more than 60 years between 1892 and 1954. Only the main building has been restored to date. There is also an interesting museum on immigration. *Daily 9:30am–3:30pm | Statue Cruises, Battery Park point of departure, ferry every 30 minutes | admission $18, including audio tour | expect delays up to one hour for security reasons; no large bags permitted | www.libertyellisfoundation. org | subway: 1 South Ferry (only board the front five carriages!)*

▣6 MUSEUM OF JEWISH HERITAGE (142 A5) *(𝄞 A17)*

"A living memorial to the Holocaust": this museum's hexagonally shaped granite building – representative of the Star of David and as a tribute to the six million Jews who lost their lives in the Holocaust – is located in Manhattan's south end. The exhibits include items from everyday life and concentration camp life as well as video presentations and documentaries.

Ellis Island – the gateway to the new world for new immigrants until 1954

Sun–Tue, Thu 10am–5:45pm, Wed 10am–8pm, Fri and before Jewish holidays 10am–3pm | 36 Battery Place | admission $12 | www.mjhnyc.org | subway: 1 South Ferry, 4, 5 Bowling Green

7 NATIONAL MUSEUM OF THE AMERICAN INDIAN ●
(142 B5) (*⊞ A18*)

A tribute to Native Americans. The New York banker George Gustav Heye collected everyday items: horse decoration, tee-pees, clothing and much more, on display in the historic U.S. Custom House. Also has changing exhibitions showcasing young American Indian artists as well as a souvenir shop. *Fri–Wed 10am–5pm, Thu 10am–8pm | 1 Bowling Green | admission free | www.nmai.si.edu | subway: 1 South Ferry, 4, 5 Bowling Green*

8 ONE WORLD TRADE CENTER ★
(142 B3–4) (*⊞ A16*)

This skyscraper (541 m/1,776 ft) points like an arrow into the sky, standing as a replacement for the Twin Towers. The observation deck located on the 100th to 102nd floors of this tallest building in the western world offers amazing views of Manhattan. The 47-second lift ride is an adventure itself as the walls of the car, which look like windows, show the development of Manhattan over time – 500 years flash by in no time at all. *May–beginning of Sept daily 9am–midnight, beginning of Sept–April 9am–8pm | Fulton Street 285 | entrance West Street | admission $32 | oneworldobservatory.com | subway: A, C, J, 2, 3, 4, 5, Fulton Street*

9 THE SKYSCRAPER MUSEUM
(142 A5) (*⊞ A17*)

Showcasing the rich architectural history of Manhattan's famous skyline, the museum's polished steel floors and ceilings spectacularly illuminate the photographs and models of its skyscrapers. The last remaining original architectural model of the World Trade Center is also housed here. *Wed–Sun noon–6pm | 39 Battery Place | admission $5 | www.skyscraper. org | subway: R, 1 Rector Street, 4, 5 Bowling Green*

10 ST PAUL'S CHAPEL
(142 B4) (*⊞ B16*)

This small chapel has been a beacon of hope since 1776, mainly for sailors who were far from home. George Washington prayed here on the day of his inaugura-

TIME TO CHILL

Being a tourist in New York can be quite exhausting so allow yourself some time out to treat yourself. Why not enjoy a pedicure? There are salons all over because New Yorkers – both men and women – love to be pampered. Foot massage and small talk are inclusive. Another good option is a massage in ● *Chinatown* (see p. 34) where there is no shortage of salons offering reflexology, facials and shoulder and neck massages. The Buddhist ● *Shambhala Meditation Center* **(147 D3)** (*⊞ D10*) (*118 W 22nd Street, sixth floor | www.ny.shambhala.org*) offers an introduction to meditation on Sundays *(noon)* and Wednesdays *(6pm)* for $10. Or how about a Turkish bath in the East Village for $40: *Russian & Turkish Baths* (*268 E 10th Street | www. russianturkishbaths.com*)?

tion in 1789. It remained completely un-scathed although it is close to the World Trade Center. An exhibition of photos and personal items movingly documents the work of the church after the attack. *209 Broadway/between Vesey and Fulton Street | www.trinitywallstreet.org | subway: A, C, 1, 2, 3, 4, 5 Broadway Nassau/ Fulton Street*

■ STATEN ISLAND FERRY ★ ● ⤴
(142 B6) (*∭ B18*)

The most beautiful view of the skyline: the round trip on the ferry past the Statue of Liberty and Ellis Island – all for free. *Every 30 minutes during the day (every 15 minutes in rush hour), hourly 11:30pm– 5:30am | 4 South Street/Whitehall Street | www.siferry.com | subway: 1 South Ferry (only the first five front carriages)*

■ STATUE OF LIBERTY ★ ⤴
(158 C4) (*∭ a21–22*)

Since 1886 "Lady Liberty" has directed her stern gaze to the east – to Europe. Erected by French sculptor Frédéric-Auguste Bartholdi as a symbol of the political ideals of the United States, the statue stands 46 m/151 ft tall (base: 47m/ 154 ft) and weighs 225 t. A limited number of day tickets are issued. Expect delays of around an hour (book online). *Ferries 9:30am– 3:30pm every 30 minutes to Liberty Island and Ellis Island from the office of the Circle Line in Castle Clinton in Battery Park | ticket $21 (including admission to the statue's crown and Ellis Island) | tel. 1 877 523 98 49 | www.statuecruises.com | subway: 1 South Ferry, 4, 5 Bowling Green*

■ STOCK EXCHANGE
(142 B5) (*∭ B17*)

Constituting the hub of the financial district is the landmark NYSE with its neo-classical architecture. The visitors' gallery is closed for security reasons. *20 Broad*

National landmark – the Statue of Liberty

Street | www.nyse.com | subway: R Rector Street, 2–5 Wall Street

■ TRIBECA
(142 B–C 1–3) (*∭ B–C 14–15*)

South of Canal Street (*Tri*angle *Be*low *Ca*nal) was once the city's market district –

Washington Market. Today its renovated warehouses have become stylish residential lofts. Partygoers roam here. There is a good chance of celebrity spotting if you have a meal at the hot spots *Nobu* and *Next Door Nobu* (see p. 64). *Subway: 1 Franklin Street*

15 WALL STREET
(142 B–C5) (*መ B17*)

This small street at Manhattan's southern tip may not be quite so famous if it wasn't the scene of the infamous Wall Street Crash in October 1929. "Black Thursday" ("Black Friday" in Europe because of the time difference) saw the *New York Stock Exchange* become a symbol of both might and misery. There are good reasons why one of the groups of activists that criticise the goings-on in the Financial District is called Occupy Wall Street. *Subway: 2–5 Wall Street*

CHINATOWN, LITTLE ITALY & SOHO

New York's ethnic diversity is particularly apparent in these districts. The unfamiliar smells, exotic foods and colourful buzz in the streets are so authentic that you will feel as though you have travelled to another continent without ever leaving the city.

A host of Chinese grocery stores, pizzerias, high-end boutiques, pricey galleries, Vietnamese restaurants and Italian cafés all capture the imagination and tempt you to try all there is on offer. Almost half of New York's 300,000 or so Chinese inhabitants live in *Chinatown* and many do not speak a word of English. Everything is signposted in Chinese. For as little as the price of a subway ticket, you can get a taste of Asia. When eating out in Chinatown bear in mind that many of its restaurants do not have a liquor license – but you can bring along your own beer or wine for a nominal corkage fee of around $3.

The Italian immigrants who settled in *Little Italy* at the beginning of the 20th century are having a hard time today. A flood of new immigrants to Chinatown means that it is encroaching across the old Canal Street border. Yuppies are moving into the expensive apartments and tourists throng the streets. But, you can still order a good cappuccino in a street café and drink in some Italian atmosphere. To the west of

Power and brass: Wall Street

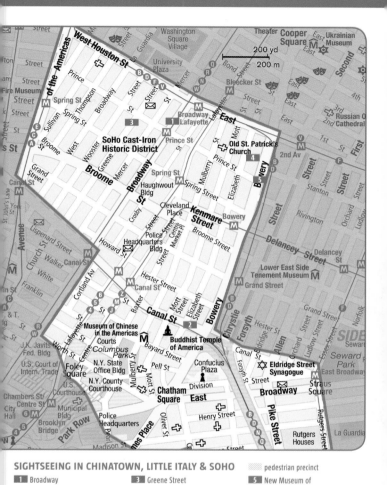

SIGHTSEEING IN CHINATOWN, LITTLE ITALY & SOHO

▨ pedestrian precinct

1 Broadway
2 Canal Street
3 Greene Street
4 Int. Center of Photography
5 New Museum of Contemporary Art

Little Italy lies *SoHo*. The name stands for *South of Houston Street* and this district between Broadway and Avenue of the Americas was discovered by artists at the start of the 1970s. Galleries and boutiques soon followed suit. Today SoHo is New York's shoppers' paradise, if a pricey one.

1 BROADWAY (142 B5) (ℳ A17)
Cutting right through the middle of New York is not only its most famous street, but also its longest: Broadway. It runs from the southernmost tip of Manhattan and stretches over 13 miles north. Broadway is the only diagonal street in the city's

otherwise straight-line grid. It winds its way from the East Side straight through Midtown to Upper West Side and to Harlem. In SoHo, shopping on Broadway has the added appeal of art galleries and cut-price jeans emporiums alongside designer boutiques. Times Square is the centre of the vibrant nightlife of the Theater District. *Subway: B, D, F, M Broadway-Lafayette*

■2 CANAL STREET (142 B1 (*᳄ B14*)
Canal Street separates the two districts of West Village and SoHo from neighbouring TriBeCa and this is also where Little Italy borders on Chinatown. The best way to get to know it is to take a Saturday stroll from 6th Avenue in an easterly direction towards Manhattan Bridge. Almost everything is for sale here. Chinatown also has all the fish and vegetables stores for which even Uptowners will make the trip downtown. *Subway: A C, E, N, Q, R Canal Street*

■3 GREENE STREET
(142 C2–143 D1) (*᳄ C14*)
SoHo is also known for its well-preserved cast iron buildings. The historic area is characterised by the ornate and decorative facades from the 19th century. Its narrow cobbled streets also enhance the atmosphere of the industrial-style architecture. There are about 50 houses, all with high ceilings and sleek supporting columns, which have been preserved. Most are in Greene Street between Canal and Prince Street. *Subway: A C, E, N, Q, R Canal Street*

■4 INTERNATIONAL CENTER OF PHOTOGRAPHY (143 E1) (*᳄ D14*)
This hip photo museum puts on changing exhibitions by well-known photographers and talented newcomers. Videos, art, projects, photo reportages, talks - all of this happens here. Not forgetting the cosy café and an exciting shop. *Tue–Thu 10am–6pm, Fri–Sun 10am–8pm | admission $14, Fri 5am–8pm admission with a voluntary donation | 250 Bowery | www.icp.org | subway: J, Z Bowery*

■5 NEW MUSEUM OF CONTEMPORARY ART
(143 E2) (*᳄ D14*)
Has someone piled up outsized shoe boxes? To match the exterior of Manhattan's most innovative museum architecture, inside you will find the very latest avant-garde art. The exhibitions are an exciting complement to the gallery districts of SoHo, Lower East Side and

LOW BUDGET

● *Big Apple Greeters (tel. 1212 6 69 81 59 | bigapplegreeter.org)* are enthusiastic New Yorkers who volunteer to show tourists their city in their spare time – free of charge. These very personal tours are quite popular and it is a good idea to book well in advance.

The free weekly newspaper *Village Voice* is the city's events calendar with comprehensive arts and culture listings. Look out for the red boxes at the side of the street and in some cafés. *www.villagevoice.com*

If you are adventurous and the idea of seeing New York from the water appeals, then you can rent a free kayak from *Downtown Boathouse (opening hours: see website | pier 96 at 56th Street in the Hudson River Park or 72nd Street in Riverside Park, go down the steps to the water | www.downtownboathouse.org).*

Walking along Canal Street is like taking a trip to China

Chelsea, where you will also find contemporary art – but free of charge. The museum also has a café and shop. *Wed, Fri–Sun 11am–6pm, Thu 11am–9pm | 235 Bowery/corner Prince Street | admission $12 | www.newmuseum.org | subway: Broadway-Lafayette, B, D, F, M*

GREENWICH VILLAGE, EAST VILLAGE & LOWER EAST SIDE

Until the 1960s, Greenwich Village was the domain of writers, poets, dancers, artists, students and professors from New York University.

Today it has evolved into an expensive residential area spared from skyscrapers. Many of its houses still have their magnificent staircases of yesteryear. Some of the brownstones or terraced buildings and town houses date back to the 19th century. Quite uncharacteristic for Manhattan here the narrow streets have names, not numbers. East of Greenwich is *East Village* popular among young people.

The old Jewish, Polish and Russian district between the Bowery and Avenue A as well as between 1st and 12th Streets used to be a colourful bohemian artists' district. However, rising rents and increasing gentrification have forced many artists to move out to Brooklyn and Queens. Street chic is still very much in vogue here and it is an excellent place to eat as there are many reasonably priced ethnic restaurants representing a mix of different nationalities such as Tibetan, Arabic and Greek.

The *Lower East Side* became famous – and infamous – as the home of many of the European immigrants that arrived in the city at the end of the 19th century. The

Tenement Museum documents the appalling living conditions the immigrants endured in their new homeland. Today, the district is fresh, dynamic, exciting and energetic with its galleries, quaint designer shops and unconventional bars.

◼ CHRISTOPHER STREET
(146 B–C5) (*ᗰ B–C12*)

In the heart of Greenwich Village lies the hub of New York's gay community with pubs, bars, bookstores and restaurants where New York's gays and lesbians meet. *Subway: 1 Christopher Street*

◼ FIFTH AVENUE ★
(147 D5) (*ᗰ D13*)

Here, all of New York's large parades take place (e.g. the Thanksgiving Parade and the Saint Patrick's Day Parade). It is also where New York showcases its crème de la crème of glamorous boutiques and department stores (e.g. Tiffany and Bergdorf Goodman), superb museums (e.g. Metropolitan Museum and Guggenheim Museum) and architectural innovations (e.g. the Rockefeller Center and the Empire State Building). You will soon notice that Fifth Avenue, which begins in the south on Washington Square, serves as an important orientation point in this concrete jungle: It halves Manhattan's numbered streets into West (W) and East (E).

◼ OLD MERCHANT'S HOUSE
(147 D6) (*ᗰ D13*)

The house of an affluent ironmonger is the city's only one from the 19th century whose interior is still intact. *Fri–Mon noon–5pm | 29 E 4th Street/between Lafayette Street and Bowery | admission $10 | www.merchantshouse.com | subway: 6 Astor Place*

Fifth Avenue – synonymous with Manhattan's best addresses

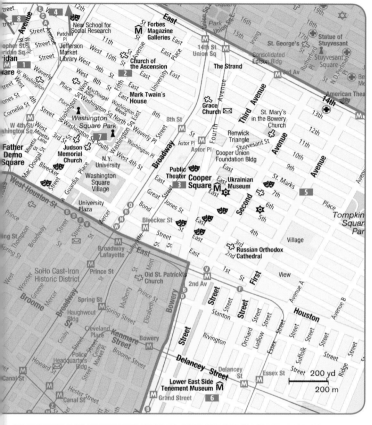

SIGHTSEEING IN GREENWICH VILLAGE, EAST VILLAGE & LOWER EAST SIDE

1 Christopher Street
2 Fifth Avenue
3 Old Merchant's House
4 Rubin Museum of Art
5 St Marks Place
6 Tenement Museum
7 Washington Square
8 Whitney Museum of American Art

4 RUBIN MUSEUM OF ART ●
(146 C3) (*ad* D11)

The Dalai Lama would love it: the museum exhibits Buddhist art from the Himalayas – paintings from Bhutan, fabrics from China, sculptures from Tibet, some of it centuries old, some of it brand new.

Round off your visit with a cocktail, a salad or an Asian snack in the trendy bar. *Mon, Thu 11am–5pm, Wed 11am–9pm, Fri 11am–10pm, Sat, Sun 11am–6pm | 150 W 17th Street/between 6th Av. and 7th Av. | admission $15 | www.rmanyc.org | subway: F, L, M 14th Street*

MIDTOWN

5 ■ ST MARKS PLACE
(147 E–F6) (*∅ E13*)

Would you like to rummage through secondhand clothes, buy cheeky T-shirts and take a break in restaurants like *Ukrainian (140 2nd Av.)*, where they serve Ukrainian specialities, or in *Veselka (144 2nd Av.)*, a favourite spot for night owls thanks to its 24-hour service? Then come to this quarter, where Polish and Ukrainian immigrants settled for decades. By the way: 8th Street is called St Marks Place here. *Subway: F 2 Av.*

6 ■ INSIDER TIP ▶ TENEMENT MUSEUM
(143 E2) (*∅ E15*)

Victoria is 14 years old and comes – from the 19th century. The story that this Greek immigrant tells you is only one of many imaginative tours of this impressive museum devoted to the living conditions of poor New Yorkers in the 1800s. *Daily 10:30am–5pm | 103 Orchard Street | admission $25 | bookings essential: tel. 1 212 9 82 84 20 | www.tenement.org | subway: F Delancey Street*

7 ■ WASHINGTON SQUARE
(146 C5–147 D5) (*∅ D13*)

Jugglers, mime artists and rap dancers: take the stage! Washington Arch was built to commemorate the centennial of the inauguration of the first American president George Washington. Previously it had been used as a public burial ground and for public hangings. Today street musicians, children, joggers and students from New York University all vie for a spot in the sun on the lawns. *Subway: A–F, M W 4 Street*

8 ■ WHITNEY MUSEUM OF
AMERICAN ART (146 B3) (*∅ B11*)

The acclaimed museum building is designed by the architect Renzo Piano and located in the Meatpacking District next to the High Line. The ingenious architecture is not only a home for 20th-century American art, but is remarkable for its galleries bathed in light and terraces with stunning views of New Jersey, the Hudson River and Manhattan. Its collection includes excellent works by Georgia O'Keefe, Edward Hopper, Roy Lichtenstein, Andy Warhol and Jasper Johns. Every two years during May it hosts the much-discussed *Whitney Biennale of American Art,* an insightful inventory, as it were, of the cutting-edge art, mostly by young artists. The museum shop sells art books, a restaurant is located on the ground floor and a café on the roof. *Mon, Wed/Thu 10:30am–6pm, Fri/Sat 10:30am–10pm | 99 Gansevoort Street | admission $22, Fri 7pm–10pm admission with a voluntary donation | whitney.org | subway: A, C, E L 14th Street*

MIDTOWN

Midtown is where people rush along the streets between skyscrapers: this is a working district.

But you are in no hurry – what a luxury! Take time to admire the splendours of the art-deco Chrysler Building and the renovated Grand Central Terminal, the stylish luxury apartment blocks and some remarkable museums that you can visit here. At night take in a musical, jazz concert or the opera in the Theater District.

1 ■ BRYANT PARK
(151 D6) (*∅ F8*)

Yes, this is modern Manhattan: a park with WiFi! If you don't want to use the fast broadband connection, you can play chess or table tennis. Put your children on the horses of the French carousel, or watch a movie outdoors in the evening. In this green gem between the skyscrapers, taking a break is always fun. *42nd St betwen 5th and 6th Av. | www. bryantpark.org | subway: B, D, F, M 42 St-Bryant Pk.*

2 CHRYSLER BUILDING
(148 A1) (*M* G9)

An all time favourite skyscraper among New Yorkers themselves, this magnificent art-deco building dates back to 1930. Even though the rooftop area is off limits, a visit to its lobby with its marble floors, murals and 18 lifts – with doors manufactured from a variety of woods – is well worth it. Built by architect William van Alen for the Chrysler motor vehicle group, its elegant and distinctive exterior was a play on the chrome-laden features of the Chrysler cars like the radiator grill and bonnet or hood. *405 Lexington Av./between 42nd and 43rd Street | subway: 4–7, S Grand Central*

3 EMPIRE STATE BUILDING ★ 🔆
(147 E2) (*M* E9)

102 storeys high and built of concrete, limestone and granite with a steel frame, the Empire State Building stands 443 m/ 1,454 ft tall (to the end of its lightning conductor) and is one of the city's key landmarks. At night it is floodlit – on the fourth of July in red, white and blue to mark Independence Day. It was inaugurated in 1931 after a construction time of only 18 months. Take a closer look at the beautiful marble and bronze inlays in the lobby on your way to the *Ticket Office (entrance in 34th Street)*. The view from the *observatory* on the 86th floor reached by high-speed lifts will make for an absolutely memorable experience. If the sky is clear you can see for 50 miles. Come prepared for lengthy delays because of security checks! 🌐 The building has been converted to fulfil stringent ecological criteria which resulted in a 40 per cent

Checkmate on Washington Square – it's anyone's game

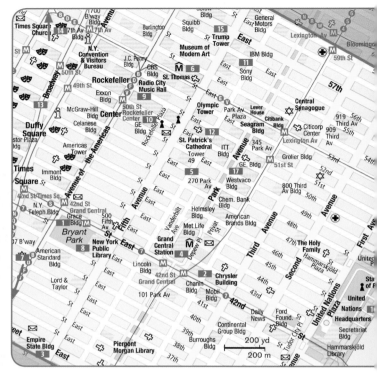

SIGHTSEEING IN MIDTOWN

1 Bryant Park
2 Chrysler Building
3 Empire State Building
4 Grand Central Terminal
5 Madison Avenue
6 Museum of Modern Art
7 Museum of Sex
8 New York Public Library
9 Radio City Music Hall
10 Rockefeller Center
11 Sony Building/550 Madison Avenue
12 St Patrick's Cathedral
13 Theater District
14 Time Warner Center
15 Trump Tower
16 United Nations
17 Waldorf-Astoria

energy saving. The Skyride simulator is not worth trying: the "attraction" is outdated and too expensive at an additional $27. *Daily 8am–2am | 350 5th Av./34th Street | admission $34 for 1st observation deck (86th floor), $54 for both decks (86th and 102nd floors), express tickets $60/* $80 | www.esbnyc.com | subway: B, D, F, M, N, Q, R 34 Street-Herald Square*

4 GRAND CENTRAL TERMINAL
(148 A1) (∅ F9)

Some 88 million cubic feet of soil had to be excavated, 25 km (15 miles) of railway tracks repositioned and around 18,000 tons of steel processed to build this massive train station in 1913. More than 150,000 people attended the launch of the Grand Central Terminal as it is officially called over a century ago. Today the terminal only serves commuter trains from the suburbs. Its cavernous main concourse area is bigger than the nave of the Notre Dame cathedral in Paris, its façade embellished with Beaux Arts elements. Above the up to 25 m/82 ft high windows is a ceiling painted with 2,500 stars. Restaurants and snack bars (in the basement) as well as many shops fill the arcades. From the gallery level, you've got a great view, for example from the restaurants *Michael Jordan's Steakhouse* and *Cipriani Dolci* – or from the *Apple Store.*

Aside from the free INSIDER TIP *Municipal Art Society of New York's tour* of Grand Central *(daily 12:30pm | meet at the entrance to track 29/Main Concourse | $25 | tel. 1 212 9 35 39 60 | www.mas.org)* there is also the free 90 minute INSIDER TIP tour of Grand Central and the surrounding neighbourhood *(Fri 12:30pm | meet at the atrium at 120 Park Av./42nd Street | tel. 1 212 8 83 24 20 | www.grandcentralpartner ship.org)*. Subway: 4–7, S Grand Central

5 MADISON AVENUE
(147 E3) *(ᗰ E11)*

The 1960s was the golden age of the "Mad Men", the "Men of Madison Avenue". There has rarely been so much smoking, drinking and machismo on display as in the offices portrayed in the cult TV series of this name (2007–2015). This view of the world of the New York advertising business, for which Madison Avenue is still a synonym and the top address, is said to have been faithful to the reality. Today, stroll along the avenue between 44th and 86th Street to look at the stores of European couturiers and the higher-class American fashion labels: cool, fancy, eye-wateringly expensive.

6 MUSEUM OF MODERN ART ★
(152 A4–5) *(ᗰ G7)*

Manhattan's bastion of art covers an area of 650,000 sq ft. The foyer alone stretches across an entire block from 53rd Street to 54th Street. Many regard the museum

An icon among skyscrapers: the Empire State Building

as the world's best because it gives the visitor a overview of 20th-century art thanks to masterpieces by Henri Matisse, Vincent Van Gogh, Frida Kahlo and Pablo Picasso. It offers an excellent cross section of the art epochs: cubism, expressionism, futurism, post-impressionism, constructivism and surrealism. Big names like Monet, Mondrian, Kandinsky, Klee and Miró are on display as well as outstanding contemporary exhibitions. Since 1929 the museum has collected 200,000 top-quality works. You will only see a fraction of them – and after the marathon viewing you will be delighted by the sculpture garden, where you can sit on elegant chairs next to Picasso's sculpture of a goat and recharge your batteries in the sunshine. *The Modern (www.themodernnyc.com | Expensive)* housed in the museum is a restaurant with an excellent reputation although somewhat pricey. *Sat–Thu 10:30am–5:30pm, Fri 10:30am–8pm | 11 W 53rd Street/between 5th and 6th Av. | admission $25,* ● *entrance free Fri 4pm–8pm | www.moma.org | subway: B, D, F, M 47–50 Street*

7 ■ MUSEUM OF SEX (147 E2) *(ΩΩ E10)*
Things get hot on Fifth Avenue a little to the south of Midtown. The Museum of Sex gives historical explanations and displays art, but is mainly devoted to erotic pleasures and the sex business. *Sun–Thu 10am–6pm, Fri/Sat 10am–9pm | admission $17.50 | 233 5th Av. (27th St.) | museumofsex.com | subway: N, R 28th St.*

8 ■ NEW YORK PUBLIC LIBRARY (151 E6) *(ΩΩ F9)*
How many films have used this venerable library as a location? So many that it almost has the status of an icon of public reading. Impressive stone lions flank the entrance to this 1911 Beaux Arts building. Its wood panelled reading room (with internet access) and exhibitions are most impressive even if you're not a local. It houses some national treasures including a handwritten annotated version of the Declaration of Independence by Thomas Jefferson, a Gutenberg bible and manuscripts by Galileo Galilei. *Mon, Thu, Fri, Sat 10am–6pm, Tue, Wed 10am–8pm, Sun 1pm–5pm, guided tours Tue–Sat 11am*

PARK ISLAND WITH GIANT WHEEL

A garbage tip almost became the tallest hill on the east coast of America: the Fresh Kills landfill on Staten Island is the biggest man-made mound ever. After its closure in 2001, it was opened again just once more – to take the rubble from the destruction of the World Trade Center. Now Fresh Kills is being transformed. By 2030 it willll have become a park, with an area of 890 ha three times as big as Central Park. For this purpose the layers below were sealed, and beneath the heap of rubbish, from which archaeologists collected masses of information about New Yorkers' consumer behaviour, runs a network of pipes to collect methane for heating. For a long time, Fresh Kills dominated the image of Staten Island – unjustly, as the borough is green, has many beaches and lots of atmosphere. And soon it will get something even taller: the *New York Wheel (opening in 2018 | newyorkwheel.com)* will be the third-highest giant wheel in the world at 192 m/630 ft.

A library visit with style – the New York Public Library is full of atmosphere

and 2pm, Sun 2pm | 5th Av./between 40th and 42nd Street| www.nypl.org | subway: B, D, F, M 42 Street

9 RADIO CITY MUSIC HALL
(151 E5) (*ꝏ F7*)

Art deco is what defines the character of this concert hall in Rockefeller Center, seating an audience of 6,000. When it first opened its doors in 1932, it was the world's biggest. Today such varied artists as Rufus Wainwright, New Order and Joe Bonamassa give concerts here, and the Christmas show with the Rockettes, the house ballet ensemble, has its own special charm. *Viewing daily 10am–5pm | 1260 Av. of the Americas/between 50th and 51st Street | admission $24 | tickets tel. 1 212 2 47 47 77 | www.radiocity.com | subway: B, D, F, M 47–50 Street*

10 ROCKEFELLER CENTER ⭐
(151 E5) (*ꝏ F7*)

In the 1930s, oil tycoon John D. Rockefeller Jr had 228 houses torn down in New York to build a city within a city. Forming part of the complex are 14 skyscrapers – among them the 70-storey-high *Comcast Building* (the former *General Electric Building),* squares, gardens, the *Radio City Music Hall, Christie's* auction house and the broadcaster *NBC.* The ↘↙ viewing platform *Top of the Rock (admission $34| www.topoftherocknyc. com)* on the 70th floor offers spectacular views across midtown Manhattan and Central Park.

At the heart of the complex lies the world-famous ice rink that doubles up as a café on the square in the summer. In December this is where New York's iconic 20 m/50 ft illuminated Christmas tree stands tall. Check the internet *at the end of November* for the grand lighting of the tree. If you are interested in old plans, models and photos then head to the *Rockefeller Center Museum* in the basement. Free maps to tour the whole Rockefeller Center are available in the lobby. *30 Rockefeller Plaza/between 49th and 50th Street | www.rockefellercenter.com | subway: B, D, F, M 47–50 Street*

🔟 SONY BUILDING/550 MADISON AVENUE (152 A4) (𝄞 G7)

It will probably be a little while before the Sony name ceases to be associated with one of the leading postmodern skyscrapers, designed by the New York architect Philip Johnson and clad in pink granite. It is always worth taking a glance into the lobby of this high-rise with a semicircular cut-out in its diagonal roof, even if *Sony Style (www.sony.com/square-nyc)*, that paradise for lovers of electronics, has moved to lower Madison Avenue. *550 Madison Av./between 55th and 56th Street | subway: N, R 5th Av./59 Street*

🔢 ST PATRICK'S CATHEDRAL (151 F5) (𝄞 G8)

The largest Catholic church of the States offers room for 2,500 people. A tranquil spot to seek solace from the hustle and bustle of 5th Avenue at any time of day! The neo-Gothic cathedral built from stone and marble was dedicated to the Irish patron saint in 1879 and is the seat of New York's Catholic archdiocese. *5th Av./50th Street | subway: B, D, F, M 47–50 Street*

🔢 THEATER DISTRICT (151 D–E5) (𝄞 E7)

This is the place to celebrate New Year. Hundreds of thousands of New Yorkers traditionally come to Times Square on 31 December at midnight. The neon advertisements flash every night, a backdrop for theatregoers making their way to a show.

"Restaurant Row" in 46th Street (between 8th and 9th Avenue) is where everyone heads to for a meal afterwards. *Subway: N, R, S, 1–3, 7, Q 42 Street/Times Square*

14 TIME WARNER CENTER
(151 D–E3) (*∅ F6*)

229 m/751 ft high are the twin towers of the Time Warner Center. The Time Warner Group has its headquarters in this 2.8 million sq ft luxury complex. The building includes the *Hotel Mandarin Oriental*, exclusive apartments, a penthouse worth $45 million, high-end stores, the Lincoln Center's jazz auditoriums and *Per Se* (see p. 64), the most sought after restaurant in the city. *10 Columbus Circle | subway: A–D, 1 59Street-Columbus Circle*

15 TRUMP TOWER
(152 A4) (*∅ G7*)

Donald Trump built himself a monument in 1983, when he was still a scandal-plagued property developer and not yet president of the USA. This 200 m/663 ft tall apartment building has 68 floors and is renowned for its bold foyer: Five floors lined with unique orange marble, bronze ornaments, gold escalators, mirrors and an illuminated waterfall – stylish or pompous? The foyer is occupied by luxury stores for people without a credit card limit. *725 5th Av./between 56th and 57th Street | subway: N, R 5 Av./59 Street*

16 UNITED NATIONS
(148 B–C1) (*∅ H9*)

A meeting place for the whole world: This complex of four skyscrapers (1953) is the United Nations headquarters as well as the seat of several of its organisations such as Unesco and Unicef. Join a guided tour of the art exhibitions from around the world in the foyer and the imposing hall where the General Assembly meets once a year. *Tours Mon–Fri 9am–4:30pm, Sat/Sun 10am–4:30pm | United Nations Plaza, 1st Av./46th Street | admission $16 | www. un.org/tours | subway: 6 51 Street*

There might be higher lookout points, but the terrace of Rockefeller Center is something special

17 WALDORF-ASTORIA
(151 F5) (*∅ G8*)

The luxury hotel built in the art-deco style of the 1930s offered its well-to-do guests of yesteryear a very unusual special service: the hotel had its own platform as part of Grand Central Terminal. Traces of the hotel's splendour of yore only really remain in its opulent ballrooms. *301 Park Av./between 49th and 50th Street | www. waldorfastoria.com | subway: 6 51st Street*

UPTOWN & CENTRAL PARK

Uptown is for the affluent, elegant and well-educated in New York – for those who have succeeded in life.

This is probably an oversimplification and increasingly no longer valid because of the number of successful people who are now moving south into one of the expansive trendy lofts in TriBeCa or live in pretty Greenwich Village. Nevertheless, on Upper East and Upper West Side you can see impressive architecture, visit many of the large museums and get a fleeting impression of the everyday life of rich New York families. Here it is a common sight to see the nanny taking the baby for a stroll while mom and dad dedicate their days to pursuing a career somewhere in the city. The uniformed doorman opens up for you when you come home and calls a taxi when you leave again for meetings and briefings.

The area between the Hudson and Central Park is called *Upper West Side*. Columbus Avenue has one exclusive boutique next to another, while Amsterdam Avenue is a lively restaurant mile. On Broadway you will come across traditional gourmet shops like *Zabar's*. The Museum of Natural History and the Lincoln Center housing the Metropolitan Opera are the cultural attractions here. *Upper East Side*

A green oasis, in autumnal red: on Central Park Bridge

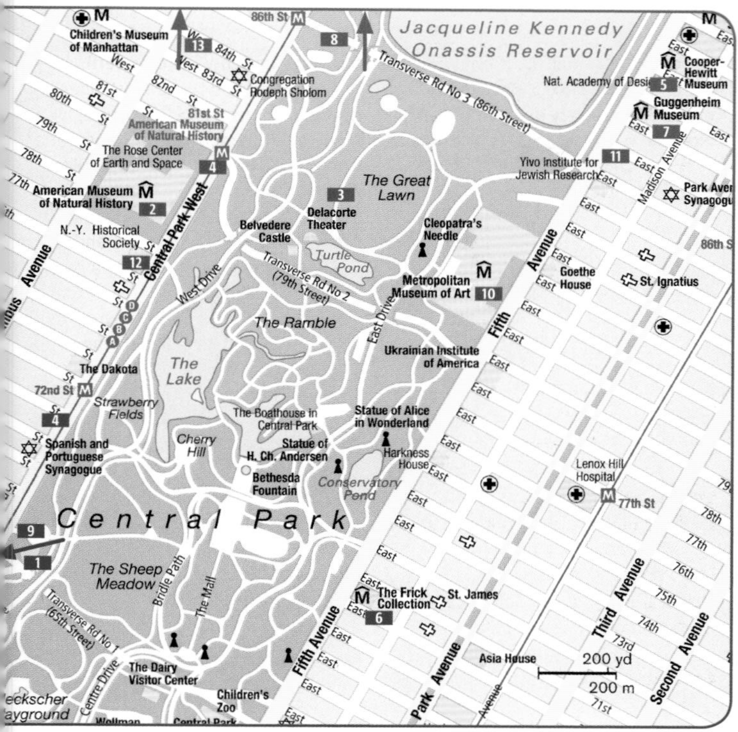

SIGHTSEEING IN UPTOWN & CENTRAL PARK

- 1 American Folk Art Museum
- 2 American Museum of Natural History
- 3 Central Park
- 4 Central Park West
- 5 Cooper-Hewitt Museum
- 6 Frick Collection
- 7 Guggenheim Museum
- 8 Harlem
- 9 Lincoln Center
- 10 Metropolitan Museum of Art
- 11 Neue Galerie New York
- 12 New York Historical Society
- 13 St John the Divine

is traditionally more conservative than its western counterpart. The district between Central Park and East River has to a large extent been upmarket in character since the end of the 19th century. The Metropolitan Museum and the Guggenheim Museum are located here, as are expensive boutiques and several high-end hotels.

1 AMERICAN FOLK ART MUSEUM

(151 E2) (*F7*)

Craft work is in vogue again, and here in the museum you will find saddlecloths for Indian chiefs and quilts, those artistic bedspreads made from hundreds of patches of cotton that the wives of early American settlers made with such skill, as well as many more items of folk art and

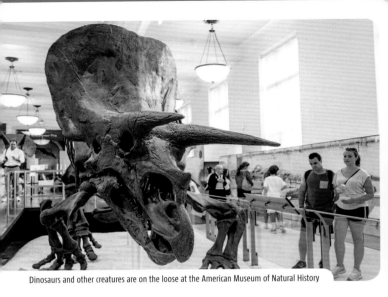

Dinosaurs and other creatures are on the loose at the American Museum of Natural History

crafts. Don't miss the museum shop – it's wonderful! *Tue–Thu, Sat 11:30am–7pm, Fri noon–7:30pm, Sun noon–6pm | 2 Lincoln Square/66th Street | admission free | www.folkartmuseum.org | subway: 1 66 Street*

🔢 AMERICAN MUSEUM OF NATURAL HISTORY ⭐ (154 C6) (*𝄜 G3*)

A 30 m/98 ft-long blue whale skeleton is suspended above you, and you get the feeling of walking through a huge aquarium. This is not the only attraction in the museum, which will leave you wide-eyed in wonder. It holds 36 million objects, among them the biggest sapphire (563 carat), the largest meteorite and the most comprehensive collection of dinosaur skeletons.

You can gain insights into the way the original inhabitants of the American continent lived. The *Hall of Biodiversity* covers the topic of how different organisms came into being, while *Habitats of the World* introduces the visitor to new ecosystems. The Imax cinema has New York's biggest big screen. An absolute must is the computerised lightning-speed space flight through our vast universe in the *Rose Center for Earth and Space.* The *Dark Universe* takes you through the Milky Way. In the *Big Bang Theater* you will be able to observe the dawn of the universe through the glass floor. Children between the ages of six and 13 can even spend a night in the museum: the exciting "sleepover" takes place once a month. *Daily 10am–5:45pm | Central Park West/79th Street | admission with a voluntary donation of $22, $27 for a combination ticket to include special exhibition or IMAX film | www. amnh.org | subway: B, C 81st Street*

🔢 CENTRAL PARK ⭐ ●
(152 A–B 1–3) (*𝄜 F–K 1–6*)

A green giant almost twice the size of the principality of Monaco, the park stretches over 843 acres. After a planning phase that lasted two decades under Frederick Law Olmsted, the park was finally completed in 1873. New Yorkers take full advantage of it from sunrise to sunset. They jog around the reservoir and row on the lake *(from $15 with $20 in cash as a security deposit)*, hire *Citi Bike* bicycles *($12 per day, check in every 30 minutes at a bike station)* or inline skates *(Blades | 156 W 72nd Street | price $25/day | www.blades. com)*, go ice-skating in *Wollman Rink* in winter *(admission $11–25, Fri–Sun $18, skate hire $8)*, take a walk in *Central Park Zoo* or meet for coffee at the *Express Café* at the Loeb Boathouse. In summer the park stages a whole variety of concerts – anything from classical music to rock. Free of charge but you must still get yourself a ticket: *Shakespeare in the Park (tel. 1 212 9 67 75 55 | www.publictheater. org)*. ☘ Dinner al fresco at *Lakeside Restaurant* can be very romantic *(April– Oct | Loeb Boathouse | tel. 1 212 5 17 22 33 | Moderate)*. *www.centralparknyc.com | subway: A–D, 159 Street-Columbus Circle; B, C 72 Street*

◀ CENTRAL PARK WEST
(151 E3–155 E2) (𝄞 F–J 1–5)

In 1884, enterprising developers had to come up with a way to lure tenants from 5th Avenue to their vacant properties in the then unfashionable area west of the park. They decorated the interiors and came up with the innovative concept that instead of living in a home with servants the rich would rent fully serviced flats instead. One of the most notable of these was the *Dakota* on the north side of 72nd Street – the building where Beatles singer and guitarist John Lennon was shot dead by a deranged fan in 1980. Similar properties were the *Beresford (81st Street)*, the *San Remo (74th/75th Street)* and the *Hotel Des Artistes (1 W 67th Street)*. *Subway: B, C 72 Street*

◀ COOPER-HEWITT MUSEUM
(156 A–B5) (𝄞 J3)

Can't you find wallpaper that's to your taste? Then create your own! You can do this in New York's specialist museum of

FIT IN THE CITY

Jogging around the reservoir running track in Central Park or through Prospect Park in Brooklyn is an experience in itself. There is also the new Hudson River Park located on Manhattan's West Side where you can jog. The massive sports complex ● *Chelsea Piers (146 B2) (𝄞 B9) (opening times vary | day pass $60 | www.chelseapiers.com)* in line with 23rd Street offers a huge choice of keep-fit options (golfing, climbing, bowling, relaxing with pilates). In summer you can swim for free in the municipal pools in Brooklyn, Queens and Manhattan *(short. travel/new7)* and in winter you can go ice skating in Central and Bryant Parks and at the Rockefeller Center. Many of the parks offer free t'ai chi, dance and yoga courses in summer *(www.bbpc.net | www.bryantpark. org)*. One of the most unusual ways to keep fit is to dance in rollerblades to disco music in Central Park. The group meets on weekends (in line with 72nd Street) – just follow the music!

design, which has many interactive exhib-its. Today this 64-room town house built by industrialist Andrew Carnegie in 1901 houses an impressive collection of tex-tiles, furniture, glass and ceramics. *Mon–Fri, Sun 10am–6pm, Sat 10am–9pm | 2 E 91st Street/5th Av. | admission $16 | www.cooperhewitt.org | subway: 4–6 86 Street*

6 FRICK COLLECTION
(152 B2) (*∅ H5*)
Spectacular! Industrialist Henry Clay Frick's exquisite collection of art housed in his Beaux Arts palace will give you an insight into the obsession that rich Americans have with art. On display are paintings by Rembrandt, Holbein, Vermeer, Goya and Renoir as well as furniture from the ep-ochs of Louis XV and XVI. After a circuit of the rooms, sit down for a rest by the foun-tain in the courtyard. More on its chang-ing exhibitions and classical concerts *(Sun 5pm)* can be found on their homepage. *Tue–Sat 10am–6pm, Sun 11am–5pm | 1 E 70th Street/5th Av. | admission $22 includ-ing audio tour, Sun 11am–1pm admission with a voluntary donation | www.frick.org | subway: 6 68 Street*

7 GUGGENHEIM MUSEUM ★
(156 A5–6) (*∅ J3*)
The Guggenheim's extraordinary build-ing by famous architect Frank Lloyd Wright – at times described as a tea cup by its critics – is one of New York's many iconic buildings. Temporary exhibitions of modern art are on display along its upward spiralling ramp that goes up four floors from street level. Exhibits include big names like Mondrian, Brancusi and Matthew Barney. A permanent exhibition is devoted to the collection of American copper magnate Solomon Guggenheim with works by van Gogh, Monet, Degas and Picasso. The museum shop sells a beautiful selection of art books. *Sun–Wed 10am–5:45pm, Fri 10am–5:45pm, Sat 10am–7:45pm | 1071 5th Av./between 88th and 89th Street | admission $25, Sat 5:45–7:45pm admission with a voluntary donation | www.guggenheim.org | sub-way: 4–6 86 Street*

8 HARLEM (156–157 C–E 1–2) (*∅ 0*)
Harlem, founded by Dutch settlers in 1658, is cool and full of diversity. Night-clubs, new restaurants and historic houses are a great mix of attractions, and the small shops on 125th Street are a browser's paradise. When slaves later built a road to New York – Broadway – many of them stayed on. In 1920s and 1930s Harlem it became chic to listen to jazz musicians like Duke Ellington and Count Basie at the *Cotton Club (today Gospel Brunch on Sat and Sun | 656 W 125th Street | costs $43.50 | tel. 1212 6 63 79 80 | www.cottonclub-newyork. com)*. Tours: *Harlem Spirituals (tel. 1212 3 91 09 00)* or *Harlem Your Way! (tel. 1212 6 90 16 87)*. ● *Gospel services* in church on Sunday mornings are joyful occasions with full-throated singing – like live concerts that cost nothing except a contribution to the collection box, e.g. in the *Abyssinian Baptist Church (Sun 11am, no rucksacks or shorts) | 132 Odell Clark Place/W 138th Street | tel. 1212 8 62 74 74 | www.abyssinian.org)*. subway: 2, 3, A–D 125 Street

9 LINCOLN CENTER FOR THE PERFORMING ARTS
(151 D–E2) (*∅ E–F 5*)
This is the cultural heart of New York. Back in the 1960s, seven concert halls and theatres were built here. The focal point is the plaza where open-air perfor-mances are staged in the summer: salsa dancing, rock concerts, readings … You will be able to admire a magnificent tap-estry by Marc Chagall in the *Metropolitan*

Opera House (see p. 94 | backstage tours Oct–June, Mon–Fri 3:00pm | admission $25 | tel. 1212 769 70 28). Jazz at Time Warner Center's *Frederick P. Rose Hall (139 E3) (⌀ F6) (33 W 60th Street/ Broadway | www.jazz.org)* is guaranteed to set you tingling. *Between W 62nd and 65th Street as well as Columbus and Amsterdam Av. | www.lincolncenter.org | subway: 1 66 Street*

🔟 METROPOLITAN MUSEUM OF ART
● (155 E6) (⌀ H–J 3–4)

Two fountains plus many tables and chairs make the huge flight of stairs leading up to the imposing façade of the museum, founded in 1870, a great place to be. Here you can take a break before or after a tour of the Met, one of the world's biggest museums. There is little to see of the original structure as the museum has had numerous additions and its extensions have encroached into Central Park. Only a quarter of its 3.2 million items can be exhibited in its two million sq ft in floor space. Temporary exhibitions showing the work of an artist or an entire epoch are inspiring to visitors and critics alike.

Head straight to the Egyptian wing (ground floor to the right) which has the original Temple of Dendur. The structure was going to be submerged by the floodwaters of the Aswan Dam but was rescued and completely rebuilt here. There are also 20 period rooms chronicling the history of American decorative arts. Among them is the Frank Lloyd Wright Room, a living room designed and decorated by the famous architect (who wanted to dictate even the clothes his clients should wear).

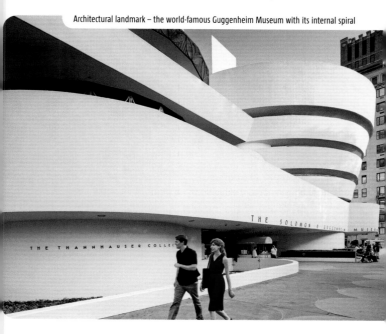

Architectural landmark – the world-famous Guggenheim Museum with its internal spiral

How about a bit of Renaissance? Masterpieces by Rembrandt, Caravaggio and El Greco hang on the first floor, but the best spot is the ● ⋰⋰ *Roof Garden*. The garden is open between April and October and should not be missed for its stunning views of Central Park and the Midtown Manhattan skyline. INSIDER TIP During summer, a bar is open until sunset on Fridays and Saturdays.

The museum is also home to Roman, Greek, Middle Eastern and Islamic art. Sections are also devoted to musical instruments, weapons, sketches, prints, photos and fashion – 40,000 garments from five centuries. On a Friday and Saturday visitors are treated to INSIDER TIP chamber music and drinks in the gallery from 4pm. *Sun–Thu 10am–5:30pm, Fri, Sat 10am–9pm | 5th Av./82nd Street | admission $25 (requested donation) | www.metmuseum.org | subway: 4–6 86 Street*

11 NEUE GALERIE NEW YORK
(156 A6) (*ω J3*)

Meaning "New Gallery" it houses German and Austrian art which had an important impact on modern American architecture and design: Gustav Klimt, Egon Schiele, Paul Klee and the "Brücke" and "Blaue Reiter" artists as well as designers of the Bauhaus school. The Viennese-style coffee shop *Café Sabarsky* serves Austrian specialities as well as the occasional *cabaret dinner. Sat–Mon, Thu, Fri 11am–6pm | 1048 5th Av./86th Street | admission $20 | www.neuegalerie.org | subway: 4–6 86 Street*

12 NEW YORK HISTORICAL SOCIETY
(154 C6) (*ω G4*)

Dating back to 1804 this is the city's oldest museum. Among the displays are photos from 1850 to the present day, a multitude of everyday items, newspapers, letters and an impressive collection of glass

The Metropolitan Museum of Art alone could be a travel destination

lamps by Louis Comfort Tiffany. *Tue–Thu, Sat 10am–6pm, Fri 10am–8pm, Sun 11am–5pm | 170 Central Park West | admission $20 | www.nyhistory.org | subway: B, C 81 Street*

⓭ ST JOHN THE DIVINE
(155 E1) (*⌘ 0*)

What may be the largest cathedral in the world has lots of space, even for dromedaries, dachshunds and kangaroos. Or for scary mummies, skeletons and monsters. You can meet the animals on the first Sunday in October, when almost 5,000 people bring their animals to be blessed in the church service. At the end of that month it's time for spooks, in one of New York's most INSIDER TIP offbeat Halloween celebrations *(7pm and 10pm | admission $25)*. Poetry readings and concerts take place all year round. The building started off in 1892 in a Byzantine and Roman style only to be continued in a neo-Gothic style in 1911. The cathedral is still unfinished. *Tours Mon 11am and 2 pm, Tue–Sat 11am and 1pm, Sun 2pm | Amsterdam Av./112th Street | admission $15 | tickets tel. 1 212 9 32 73 47 | www.stjohndivine.org | subway: 1 110th Street*

St John the Divine may be incomplete, but it is breathtaking nonetheless

OTHER DISTRICTS

BROOKLYN HEIGHTS ⚜
(139 D–E1) (*⌘ h20*)

In Brooklyn's most beautiful residential area you feel like you have stepped back into the 19th century. Located on the other end of the Brooklyn Bridge it is characterised by well preserved *brownstone* tenement buildings made of sandstone. Some of the buildings are listed. Follow Pierrepoint Street through to the Brooklyn Heights promenade which is an excellent spot for some wonderful views of Manhattan, the Brooklyn Bridge Park and Hudson River. *Subway: 2, 3 Clark Street*

BROOKLYN MUSEUM
(158 C4–159 D4) (*⌘ 0*)

New York's second largest museum is housed in this 1897 Beaux-Arts building. The *Period Rooms* showcase more than 20 New England living and dining rooms from 1675 to 1830. The American Collection offers an overview of American art. Popular exhibitions of contemporary art have pushed the museum into the spotlight in more recent times. Members of the public are invited to participate in a INSIDER **TIP** changing programme (free of charge!) every first Saturday of the month from 5 to 11 pm. It may entail anything from swing dancing lessons and portrait painting, to movie screenings, world music concerts and hip hop DJ sets. *Wed 11am–6pm, Thu 11am–10pm, Fri–Sun 11am–6pm | 200 Eastern Parkway | Brooklyn | admission $16 | www.brooklyn museum.org | subway: 2, 3 Eastern Parkway*

CARROLL GARDENS
(139 D5) (*ω g–h23*)

Today this once seedy part of Brooklyn is a sought after area with charming restaurants, delightful designer boutiques and protected heritage houses. Young families, hip couples and singles with a healthy cash flow are the kind of residents who have moved into the brownstones in Carroll Gardens and Park Slope over the past few years. American novel-

Who invented the hot dog? Supposedly it was Nathan's on Coney Island

ists like Jonathan Lethem have written about this old Italian neighbourhood that used to be popular with African-Americans and Puerto Rican families. *Subway: F, G Carroll Street*

THE CLOISTERS (159 D1) (*ω 0*)

This museum complex into which parts of four French and Spanish monasteries were integrated was built between 1934 and 1938. It is located inside Fort Tryon Park and offers an amazing view of the steep forested banks of the Hudson and the George Washington Bridge opposite it. The Metropolitan Museum's medieval art collection is housed here. *Daily 10am–5:15pm, Nov–Feb until 4:45pm | Fort Tryon Park | admission with a voluntary donation of $25 – it includes admission to the museum on the same day | www.metmuseum.org | subway: A 190 Street; bus: M 4 Cloisters/Fort Tryon Park, hop on the bus in Madison Av., between 32nd Street and 110th Street*

CONEY ISLAND
(158–159 C–D5) (*ω 0*)

The price of a subway ticket will get you to this beach known for its amusement park with listed Ferris (which has great views from the top) and the *Thunderbolt* rollercoaster from 2014. Up to half-a-million people head to the peninsula on weekends. They eat hot dogs at Nathan's or visit the *New York Aquarium* (see p. 123), where the latest attraction, Ocean Wonders: Sharks!, a huge aquarium containing almost 2 million litres of water, will probably be opened in 2018. *1208 Surf Av. | Brooklyn | subway: D, F, Q, N Coney Island, Brighton Beach*

DUMBO � (143 E–F6) (*ω E18*)

The acronym stands for *Down Under the Manhattan Bridge Overpass*. It is one of the areas in Brooklyn that have undergone dramatic changes. Factories have been converted into apartments with idyllic views of Manhattan, and there are many galleries, design stores and popular bars such as *Superfine (Sun brunch with live music | 126 Front Street | tel. 1 718 2 43 90 05 | subway: F York Street).*

The INSIDER**TIP** *Brooklyn Bridge Park* along the East River is the longest waterfront park in New York with a temporary swimming pool, outdoor cinema, beach volleyball courts, kayaking, barbecues and many other outdoor recreational options. If you are in the mood for an ice cream then look no further than the *Brooklyn Ice Cream Factory* with New York's best view *(Fulton Ferry Landing). Subway: A, C High Street | or water taxi (www.nywatertaxi.com)*

INSIDER**TIP** **GOVERNORS ISLAND**
(159 E–F6) (*Ø O*)

Take a picnic to the fort on Governors Island! For 200 years it was closed to the public, but now anyone can laze in one of the 50 hammocks or whoosh down a 20 m/65 ft slide. There are no cars, but plenty of nature, free concerts and other activities. *28 May–25 Sept Mon–Fri 10am–6pm, Sat/Sun 10am–7pm | ferry from the tip of Manhattan | www.govis land.com | subway: 1 South Ferry*

GREENPOINT (159 D3) (*Ø K4*)

The district north of Williamsburg has been nicknamed Little Poland, although nowadays you will find alongside the immigrants from Eastern Europe also young couples, artists and students escaping Williamsburg's rising rental prices. The inviting smells of Polish *kielbasa* sausages and a growing number of beer gardens with BBQs along the East River characterise the district. So many beer gardens have sprung up in Brooklyn that the *New York Times* has jokingly written

Down under the Manhattan Bridge – the famous view in Dumbo

in an article that parts of Brooklyn now feel like Bavaria. *McCarren Park (www. mccarrenpark.com)* – in what was formerly farmland – is where you can INSIDER**TIP** swim in a renovated pool from 1936.

INSIDER**TIP** **MUSEUM OF THE MOVING IMAGE** (159 D3) (*Ø O*)

Here you can make an animated film, try out sound effects, design a flip-book or watch a movie. *Wed, Thu 10.30am–5pm, Fri 10.30am–8pm, Sat, Sun 10.30am–7pm | 36–01 35th Av./37th Street | Queens | admission adults $15, children*

$7, Fri 4pm–8pm free entrance | www.movingimage.us | subway: M, R Steinway Street

P. S. 1 CONTEMPORARY ART CENTER
☼ (159 D3) (*Ⓜ L10*)

Housed in an old school, its innovative curators have given the museum its creative, avant-garde and offbeat feel. Don't miss the view from the roof over Manhattan, especially at sunset. On Saturday evenings in summer the courtyard is where one of INSIDER TIP▶ New York's most popular parties is held. "Warm up" offers live music, drinks and installations by artists and architects *(3pm–9pm | admission $18–20)*. *Thu–Mon noon–6pm | 22–25 Jackson Av./46th Av. | Queens | admission $10 | www.ps1.org | subway: E, M 23rd Street (Ely Av.)*

RED HOOK
(138 A–B 5–6) (*Ⓜ e–f 23–24*)

This district right on the water's edge is one of New York's *final frontiers*. The film classic *On the Waterfront* – for which Marlon Brando received an Oscar in 1955 – put this working-class neighbourhood on the map. Then it was discovered by artists on the hunt for cheap rents and now property speculators are moving in and its face may change forever. The Ikea furniture chain has even built a promenade with paths here to win over local residents to its plan to build a store. In summer, weekends are the best time for outings here or come in October when the *Brooklyn Waterfront Artist Coalition (www.bwac.org)* is held at the end of Van Brunt Street. Before heading back, indulge in some chocolate cake from *Baked (359 Van Brunt Street | tel. 1 718 2 22 03 45 | Budget)* or if hunger pangs have gotten the better of you order Korean steak & eggs at *The Good Fork (391 Van Brunt Street | tel. 1 718 6 43 66 36 | www.goodfork.com | Budget)*. *Subway: A, C, F, G Jay Street-MetroTech, then bus B61 to the end of Van Brunt Street*

WILLIAMSBURG
(145 D–F 3–4) (*Ⓜ H–L 16–17*)

Once upon a time it was the summer haunt of the rich, it then became an in-

SPOTLIGHT ON SPORTS

New Yorkers love sports events and it doesn't matter if they watch them in the pub with a cold beer or live at a stadium. The baseball season runs from April to September so go and see the *New York Yankees (tickets: tel. 1 800 7 45 30 00 | www.yankee.com)* at Yankee Stadium **(159 D1)** (*Ⓜ 0*) *(Bronx)* or the *New York Mets (tickets: tel. 1 718 5 07 84 99 | www.newyorkmets.com)* at the Citi Field Stadium **(159 E3)** (*Ⓜ 0*) *(Queens)* hit some home runs. The tickets from $15 upwards are reasonably priced.

For something more elegant and faster-paced, try basketball, but at $75 the tickets are much more expensive. Basketball fans can watch the *New York Knicks (tickets: tel. 1 800 7 45 30 00 | www.nba.com/knicks)* in *Madison Square Garden* **(147 D1)** (*Ⓜ D9*) from November to May. The *Metlife Stadium* **(158 B2)** (*Ⓜ 0*) *(Meadowlands | New Jersey)* is home turf to American football's *New York Jets (www.newyorkjets.com)* and *New York Giants (www.giants.com)* from September to December.

dustrial area and today it is favoured by young, successful New Yorkers as well as being home to a 30,000-strong orthodox Jewish community. The Metropolitan Avenue and Grand Street areas have an array of eclectic restaurants and galleries with quirky, offbeat names like *Bottleneck Gallery,* as well as small book and record dealers. Bedford Avenue with its many small shops, cafés and galleries is where it is at. Meanwhile, less well-to-do hipsters have moved into neighbouring Bushwick. *Subway: L Marcy Av., Bedford Av.*

FURTHER AFIELD

HUDSON RIVER VALLEY (0) (📖 0)

A day trip in a rental car north along the Hudson River through the impressive hilly, green and forested landscape is highly recommended. Follow Route 9 to *Kykuit* and the imposing *Rockefeller Estate (May–Nov Wed–Sun | admission $25–40)*

where the 41st American Vice President, Nelson B. Rockefeller's amazing art collection awaits you.

Further north in *Hyde Park,* you can take in the 54-room Renaissance mansion of renowned 19th-century railroad magnate Frederick W. Vanderbilt, *Vanderbilt Mansion (daily 9am–5pm | www.nps.gov/vama)* along with the stately home of ex-President Franklin D. Roosevelt which is also located in Hyde Park *(daily 9am–5pm | www.nps.gov/hofr).* Hyde Park is also home to the *Culinary Institute of America (tel. 1 845 4 52 96 00 | www. ciachef.edu | Budget–Expensive).* Here the United States' talented up-and-coming chefs prepare gourmet menus in four restaurants (reservation essential!).

Viticulture also thrives in the Hudson Valley, its warm humid climate is ideal for excellent white wines, e.g. *Millbrook Vineyards (daily noon–5pm | tel. 1 845 6 77 83 83 | www.millbrookwine.com).* To end your day, pop into the picture-perfect town of *Rhinebeck* that dates back to 1686.

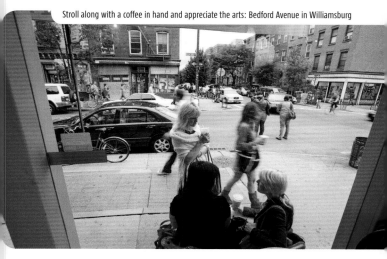

Stroll along with a coffee in hand and appreciate the arts: Bedford Avenue in Williamsburg

FOOD & DRINK

New Yorkers are always in a hurry. At midday many simply grab a sandwich and eat it standing or on the go. In the evening things get calmer.

Then it's time to choose one of the many restaurants that make New York such a seductive place. The culinary treats range from Korean *kim chi* to lobster from Maine, sushi in burritos and a juicy NY strip steak.

For those who want to get their fill quickly, there are diners, Chinese restaurants and pizza stands. Then there are the typical coffee shops, like the dinner they are a uniquely American phenomenon. They will serve you a bottomless coffee (albeit not the strongest) where you can have as many refills as you can drink for the price of just one cup. Some outlets

of this typically American way of eating out will even offer you a full breakfast for under $5. Most coffee shops serve lunch and dinner the whole day and many are open 24/7. In contrast to this, plenty of restaurants, especially the expensive ones, are closed between lunch and dinner.

It is standard practice in the United States to have a *maître de table* to show you to your table. A tip is also standard and regarded as more than just a gesture, as the tip forms a large part of your waiter's wage and the argument is that if left solely to the discretion of the patron it will not necessarily suffice (see p. 134). If not otherwise indicated, the restaurants mentioned in this travel guide are open daily for lunch and dinner. Lunch-

So many nationalities, so many cuisines! A culinary world tour from Italian and Japanese to Creole to *nouvelle american* cuisine

time is usually between noon and 2pm and dinner from 7pm to 9pm.

INSIDER TIP *Restaurant Week* in New York takes place at the end of January and in June/July and is a real attraction. For a very reasonable fixed price you will be able to enjoy a three-course lunch *($29)* or dinner *($42)* in some of the best restaurants, excluding drinks, tax (8.875 per cent) and tip. Information on participating restaurants from *NYC Visitor Information* (tel. 1 212 4 84 12 22) or at *www.nycvisit.com/restaurantweek*.

CAFÉS

INSIDER TIP **ALMAR** ✪
(143 E6) (*Ⴑ E18*)

Sit at long wooden tables in this café in the trendy Dumbo district in Brooklyn. Maybe order a panino with prosciutto and fresh mozzarella to go with your caffè latte? With all the organic ingredients, it's a healthy experience. *Closed Sun evening | 111 Front Street | tel. 1 718 8 55 52 88 | www.almardumbo.com | subway: F York Street*

CAFÉS

AMY'S BREAD ● ◉ (146 C5) *(Ⓜ C13)*
"Devil's Food" is the name of one of the cupcakes in this bakery that uses regional, organic ingredients. The bread and cake are also devilishly good, while the coffee, baguettes and jam, and the sandwiches at midday could be called heavenly. *Daily | 250 Bleecker Street/ Leroy Street | tel. 1212 6 75 78 02 | www. amysbread.com | subway: A, B, C, D, E, F, M W 4 Street*

breakfast eggs and more than 40 kinds of sandwiches. This has been the scene here for over 90 years! *Daily | 174 5th Av./60th Street | www.eisenbergsnyc. com | subway: N, R 23 Street*

INTELLIGENTSIA
(146 B3) *(Ⓜ B11)*
In this little paradise in fast-paced Chelsea, the superb coffee comes from an old Citroën minibus. The coffee bar of the

A huge glazed banana donut with pecans is a classic at Doughnut Plant

DOUGHNUT PLANT ●
(147 D2) *(Ⓜ D 10)*
Doughnut connoisseurs swear that this is where you will get the best. Even the cushions look like the ring-shaped goodies that cops eat in every self-respecting crime film. *Daily | 220 W 23rd Street | tel. 1212 5 05 37 00 | www.doughnutplant. com | subway: 1, C, E 23 Street*

EISENBERG'S SANDWICH SHOP
(147 E3) *(Ⓜ E11)*
Simply sit at the counter and watch how the cooks prepare soup, burgers, salads,

High Line Hotel is not large, but you can sit by the hedge outside, in front of the hotel and behind it! *Daily 7am | 180 Tenth Av./between 20. and 21. St. | tel. 1212 9 29 38 88 | thehighlinehotel.com | subway: C, E 23 Street*

VENIERO'S (147 E6) *(Ⓜ E13)*
Vibrant, loud and crowded – a sweet necessity since 1894. Buy some *dolci* for your next breakfast at the counter before you go! *Daily 8am–midnight | 342 E 11th Street/between 1st and 2nd Av. | subway: L 1 Av.*

RESTAURANTS: EXPENSIVE

A VOCE (147 E3) (*ⅅ E10*)

A modern interior and delectable new Italian cuisine make for a winning combination. *Closed Sun | 41 Madison Av. | 26th Street | tel. 1212 545 85 55 | www.avocerestaurant.com | subway: 6 23 Street*

CARBONE
(146 C6) (*ⅅ C13*)

The name says Italy, the Mafia and delicious pasta. The critics say two thumbs up. The menu includes pasta with lobster, clams and caper sauce. *Sat, Sun evenings only | 181 Thompson Street/between Bleecker and W Houston Street | tel. 1212 2 54 30 00 | www.carbonenewyork.com | subway: B, D, F, M Broadway-Lafayette*

CHURRASCARIA PLATAFORMA
(151 D4) (*ⅅ E7*)

Meat – and plenty of it – grilled to perfection on a skewer. Brazilian steak house with an excellent salad bar. *Prix fixe: lunch $40, dinner all you can eat $65. Belvedere Hotel | 316 W 49th Street | tel.* 1212 2 45 05 05 | plataformaonline.com | subway: C 50 Street

CRAFT 🌀
(147 D3) (*ⅅ D11*)

The critics love Tom Colicchio who developed the concept for this upscale restaurant. Selected farmers work closely with the chef and owner to ensure that only the finest ingredients are served. *Daily | 43 E 19th Street | tel. 1212 7 80 08 80 | www.craftrestaurant.com | subway: R, 6 23 Street*

ELEVEN MADISON PARK
(147 E3) (*ⅅ E11*)

The 8- to 10-course menu with exquisite French cuisine costs $295. Three Michelin stars for seasonal dishes using local ingredients! *Daily, Sun–Wed evenings only | 11 Madison Av. | tel. 1212 8 89 09 05 | www.elevenmadisonpark.com | subway: R, 6 23 Street*

GRÜNAUER BISTRO (153 E2) (*ⅅ K5*)

Yorkville on Upper East Side was home to many German speakers in the 19th

---

⭐ **Grand Banks**
Oysters at sundown on an old cod-fishing boat with a huge wow factor.
→ p. 64

⭐ **Nougatine**
Modern French-American cuisine to die for → p. 64

⭐ **Buddakan**
Stylish décor and excellent Asian cuisine → p. 65

⭐ **The Fat Radish**
Come here for vegetarian soul food. → p. 66

⭐ **Prune**
Brunch here is amazing – eleven Bloody Mary variations to choose from → p. 67

⭐ **Schiller's Liquor Bar**
Great location in the hip Lower East Side → p. 68

⭐ **Superiority Burger**
Vegetarian, daring and cheap. Try a Sloppy Dave. → p. 71

⭐ **Pure**
Enjoy home-made noodles with Thai in this charming eatery. → p. 67

MARCO POLO HIGHLIGHTS

and early 20th century. This is a culinary trip to Austria. A pianist accompanies the Vienna schnitzel, the Austrian wines are reasonably priced and the waiters serve your goulash with polished manners. *Closed Sun, evenings only | 1578 First Av./82 Street | tel. 1212 9 88 10 77 | grunauernyc.com | subway: Q E 86 Street*

NOBU
(142 B2) (f B15)

For the *omakase* lunch menu, top chef Nobu himself selects the dishes, $75–95. Book early. Next door without a reservation: *Next Door Nobu*. *105 Hudson Street/ Franklin Street | tel. 1212 2 19 05 00 | www. noburestaurants.com | subway: 1 Franklin Street*

NOUGATINE ★ (151 E3) (*ad F6*)

Jean-Georges Vongerichten opened a restaurant and the "in" crowd followed. Whether Maine lobster or pork chops with prosciutto, the food is top-notch. *1 Central Park W | tel. 1212 2 99 39 00 | jean-georgesrestaurant.com | subway: 1, A, B, C, D 59 Street-Columbus Circle*

PETER LUGER
(142 B4) (*ad J17*)

To this day the 130-year-old steakhouse entices its guests with its charm and large portions. For 30 years this has been voted the best steakhouse in New York. Credit cards not accepted. *178 Broadway/between Driggs and Bedford Street | tel. 1 718 3 87 74 00 | www.peterluger.com | subway: J Marcy Av.*

FAVOURITE EATERIES

I'd sooner eat on a schooner

Eat oysters in fine style at ★ *Grand Banks* **(142 A2)** (*ad A15*) *(April–Oct Mon/ Tue evening | Pier 25 | Hudson River Park | www.grandbanks. org | subway: 1 Franklin Street)*, an old codfishery schooner that bobs on the waves of the Hudson River in TriBeCa. The mussels come from Long Island and the West Coast.

Fine dining

Thomas Keller will take you on a culinary journey in *Per Se* **(139 E3)** (*ad F6*) *(Daily, Mon–Thu evenings only | 10 Columbus Circle/60th Street | 4th floor | tel. 1212 8 23 93 35 | www.perseny.com | subway: A–D, 1 59 Street-Columbus Circle)*. Reservations weeks in advance. The nine-course tasting menu for $325 changes daily.

Green living

Are those hens over there? No, quail! But don't worry, the mascots of the ambitious organic restaurant ⚫ *Olmsted* **(140 C6)** (*ad M24*) *(daily from 5pm | 659 Vanderbilt Av./near Park Place | Prospect Heights | tel. 1 718 5 52 26 10 | olmstednyc.com | subway: 2, 3 Grand Army Plaza)* are not on the menu. But other foods, grown in a garden in Brooklyn (!), will find their way to your plate.

Imperial dining

Vegetarian food from Korea is a rarity, and the Emperor Tasting Menu (6 courses for $60) at *Hangawi* **(147 F2)** (*ad F10*) *(daily, Sun only in the evening | 12 E 32nd Street | tel. 1212 2 13 00 77 | www.hangawirestaurant. com | subway: 6 33 Street)* is a treat for culinary kings of Koreatown.

Nobu serves treasured Japanese delicacies, but not without a reservation well in advance

TOCQUEVILLE (141 D4) *(ØD 12)*
Upscale, contemporary American cuisine. Excellent prix fixe menu (e.g. smoked duck breast in elderflower-lychee sauce with pear) – $29 (lunch) or $135 (5-course tasting dinner). *Daily, Sun evenings only | 1 E 15th Street | tel. 1212 6 47 15 15 | www.tocquevillerestaurant. com | subway: L, N, Q, R, 4, 5, 6 14 Street-Union Square*

RESTAURANTS: MODERATE

BRYANT PARK GRILL (151 D–E6) *(ØF8)*
This restaurant in the park is where the fashionistas congregate in the open air for seafood and barbecue dishes. Brunch on weekends from 11:30 am. *25 W 40th Street/between 5th and 6th Av. | tel. 1212 8 40 65 00 | www.arkrestaurants. com | subway: B, D, F, M 42 Street*

BUDDAKAN ★
(146 B3) *(Ø C11)*
The surroundings are something like Rococo meets Asia meets futuristic,

including banquet tables and chandeliers. The modern Asian dishes are as delicious as the atmosphere is pompous. Both the décor and the food have won awards – no wonder it's hard to concentrate on your meal! *Evenings only | 75 9th Av./16th Street | tel. 1212 9 89 66 99 | www.buddakannyc.com | subway: A, C, E, L 14 Street*

INSIDER TIP CANDLE 79 ✪
(153 D2) *(Ø J5)*
Once you've eaten a (organic) vegetarian meal here, you might think about giving up meat. Saturday and Sunday brunch from noon to 3.30pm. *154 E 79th Street | tel. 1212 4 72 09 70 | www.candle79.com | subway: 6 77 Street*

COPPELIA
(146 C4) *(Ø C11)*
Cuba is in, so delight in fish tacos, empenadas and guacamole – every day, round the clock. *207 W 14th Street | near 7th Av. | tel. 1212 8 58 50 01 | coppelianyc. com | subway: 1, 2, 3 14 Street*

THE FAT RADISH ★
(143 E3) (*D16*)

On hip Lower East Side two British chefs cook healthy, elegant comfort food with fresh seasonal vegetables and organic meat – meals for the soul in charmingly designed surroundings. Buy the cookbook of the same name to take home! *Daily | 17 Orchard Street | near Canal St. | tel. 1212 3 00 40 53 | www.thefatradishnyc.com | subway: F East Broadway*

FETTE SAU
(145 D–E3) (*J16*)

Grilled organic meat with craft beer to wash it down in trendy Williamsburg. Rustic and cosy. *Mon–Wed from 5pm, Thu–Sun from noon | 354 Metropolitan Av. | tel. 1 718 9 63 34 04 | www.fettesaubbq.com | subway: L Bedford Av.*

HAN BAT (147 E1) (*E9*)

Authentic food round the clock in Korea-town. Rice with eggs, meat and vegetables from the hot stone grill, but you can also order offal, tongue or the rice dish *bi bim bab*. *53 W 35 Street/5th Av. | tel. 1212 6 29 55 88 | subway: B, D, F, M, N, O, R 34 Street-Herald Square*

LES HALLES
(142 B4) (*B17*)

Top chef Anthony Bourdain once ruled the kitchen here. Now excellent successors put on a celebration of French cuisine. If you'd like to try it for yourself, buy the house cookbook! *15 John Street | tel. 1212 2 85 85 85 | leshalles.net | subway: N, R Cordtland*

MAREA
(151 E3) (*F6*)

Seafood is celebrated in this excellent Italian restaurant serving delectable flounder, monkfish, muscles, lobsters and langoustine dishes. *240 Central Park South/Broadway | tel. 1212 5 82 51 00 | www.marea-nyc.com | subway: A–D, 1 59 Street-Columbus Circle*

MISSION CHINESE FOOD
(143 E3) (*E16*)

The green-tea noodles and the tiger salad are to die for! The out-of-the-ordinary Chinese dishes here are extremely popular, so be prepared to wait. Or arrive early. *From 5.30pm | 171 E. Broadway | tel. 1212 4 32 03 00 | missionchinesefood.com | subway: F East Broadway*

INSIDER TIP ▶ MOMOFUKU SSÄM BAR
(147 E5) (*E13*)

Popular, hip restaurant for meat fans: veal, lamb, ham and bacon all prepared Asian-style. *207 2nd Av. | 13th Street | tel. 1212 2 54 35 00 | www.momofuku.com | subway: 3 3rd Av.*

OYSTER BAR (148 A1) (*F9*)

Grand Central Terminal's Oyster Bar offers a dozen varieties of oysters, *pan roasts,* lobster soup and fish fresh from the grill. *Closed Sun | Grand Central Terminal, Lower Level between Vanderbilt and Lexington Av. | tel. 1212 4 90 66 50 | www.oyster barny.com | subway: 4–7 Grand Central*

PRUNE ⭐
(143 E1) (*⚂ E14*)

Poached eggs, Hollandaise sauce and Canadian ham make brunch *(Sat/Sun)* popular here. *54 E 1st Street/between 1st and 2nd Av. | tel. 1 212 6 77 62 21 | www.prunerestaurant.com | subway: F, M 2nd Av.*

PURE ⭐
(151 D4) (*⚂ E7*)

Take a trip to Asia for an hour or so. The recipes in this delightful small cookhouse in Hell's Kitchen with 35 seats were brought back from Thailand by Vanida Bank. *Daily | 766 Ninth Av./between 51st and 52nd St. | tel. 1 212 5 81 09 99 | www.purethaicookhouse.com | subway: C, E 50 Street*

THE REDHEAD 🌐
(147 F5) (*⚂ F13*)

Favourite meeting place for the residents of East Village in a warm atmosphere; it's always full. Its (organic) cuisine is inspired by the American southern states. Cheaper meals before 7pm. *Daily from 4pm | 349 E 13th Street/1st Av. | tel. 1 212 5 33 62 12 | www.theredheadnyc.com | subway: L 1 Av.*

ROBATAYA (147 E6) (*⚂ E13*)

Arriving guests are greeted loudly in Japanese by the staff. It is a good idea to sit right INSIDER TIP in front at the grill in the first room where you can watch the spectacle of two Kimono-clad men preparing the dishes. *231 E 9th Street | tel. 1 212 9 79 96 74 | www.robataya-ny.com | subway: 6 Astor Place, R, N 8 Street*

ROBERT ⚹
(151 E3) (*⚂ F6*)

What makes this restaurant in the Museum of Art and Design so inviting is the perfect view it affords of Columbus Circle and Central Park. Lounge on one of the comfortable couches or order a tender *New York strip steak* and enjoy a memorable New York experience. *2 Columbus Circle | tel. 1 212 2 99 77 30 | www.robertnyc.com | subway: A–D, 1 59 Street-Columbus Circle*

RUSS AND DAUGHTERS CAFÉ
(143 E2) (*⚂ E15*)

All day long, Jewish treats from eastern Europe, in old New York style: matze dumpling soup, borsht and latkes (potato cakes) with caviar. *Daily until 10pm | 27 Orchard Street/between Rivington and*

Easy to let the Oyster Bar in Grand Central Terminal derail you

LOCAL SPECIALITIES

bagel – the variations are countless, anything from sesame to onions (photo right)

carpaccio – in New York it is not the usual raw beef option but rather all kinds of raw fish

cheesecake – New York's famous version is rich, creamy and indulgent. From plain to pistachio vanilla – the variations are endless

clam chowder – clam soup – the New England version is white and the Manhattan version red (with tomatoes)

crab cakes – sure beats traditional fish cakes!

eggs – essential cholesterol boost for any American. With it come bacon (or Canadian bacon), toast and home fries

lobster – in New York lobster is served in an endless variety of ways

new york strip steak – a typical New York cut of loin (marbled with fat). Best cuts are prime rib or filet mignon

oyster – served with vinegar and pink pepper or with ketchup (photo left)

sandwiches – in New York the sandwich has a strong Jewish heritage. The *Reuben* (sauerkraut and soft cheese) and *pastrami* (a highly seasoned sliced smoked beef) are two classics. In the sandwich bars you choose the filling, the type of bread e.g. whole wheat or rye and your garnish e.g. lettuce, tomato, mayonnaise, mustard or onion

turkey – served for Thanksgiving with cranberries, gravy and sweet potatoes. Also popular as a cold meat

Delancey St. | tel. 1212 475 48 80 | www.russanddaughterscafe.com | subway: F Delancey Street

SCHILLER'S LIQUOR BAR ★
(143 F2) (*ØØ E15*)

New Yorkers love their weekend brunch, and it's truly delicious at this restaurant serving European food on Lower East Side. *131 Rivington Street/Norfolk Street | tel.*

1212 2 60 45 55 | www.schillersny.com | subway: F Delancey Street

INSIDER TIP UNITED NATIONS DINING ROOM (148 B1) (*ØØ H9*)

For $34,99 get you an opulent lunch buffet in the UN canteen. Included in the price is a fabulous view across the East River and the possibility of rubbing shoulders with famous politicians and celebrities from around the world. Remember to bring along ID (passport). Men must wear a jacket. *Lunch 11:30am–2:30pm | visitors' entrance: 1st Av. and 46th Street | reservations the day before : tel. 1 917 3 67 33 14 | www.delegatesdiningroom-un.com | subway: 4, 5, 6, 7, S Grand Central-42 Street*

RESTAURANTS: BUDGET

CITY BAKERY ⊛
(147 D4) (*ᗰ D11*)
A good lunch venue for your city expeditions with a fish, meat and vegetarian buffet with some innovative flavour combinations and produce from nearby Union Square Farmer's market. *Mon–Sat 7:30am–7pm, Sun 9am–6pm | 3 W 18th Street | tel. 1212 3 66 14 14 | www.thecity bakery.com | subway: L, N, Q, R, 4–6 14 Street-Union Square*

CHUKO (140 C5) (*ᗰ M23*)
Ramen, the savoury Japanese noodle soup, tastes so good that people are willing to queue up outside. *552 Vanderbilt Av./Dean Street | tel. 1718 5 76 67 01 | www.barchuko.com | subway: A, C Clinton-Washington Av.*

DOS TOROS TAQUERIA ⊛
Simple, fast, cheap: rustic snack bar serving tacos, burritos and quesadillas. Still, they operate sustainably, from composting leftovers to using local food. Branches in Manhattan: *11 Carmine Street (146 C5) (ᗰ C13): corner Bleecker Street | tel. 1212 6 27 20 51 | subway: A, C, E, B, D, F, M West 4 Street; 137 4th Av. (147 E5) (ᗰ E12): corner 13th Street | tel. 1212 6 77 73 00 | subway: 4–6, L, N, Q, R 14 Street-Union Square); 1111 Lexington Av. (152 C2) (ᗰ J5): corner 77th Street | tel. 1212 5 35 46 58 | subway: 6 77 Street; 200 Vesey Street (142 A3) (ᗰ A16): tel. 1212 7 86 03 92 | subway: A, C, E Chambers Street | www.dostoros.com*

ESPERANTO (144 A1) (*ᗰ F14*)
Brazilian? Caribbean? Even if you cannot put a name to it you will enjoy excellent multicultural cuisine and live music. Brunch on weekends. *145 Av. C/9th Street | tel. 1212 5 05 65 59 | www.esperantony. com | subway: 6 Astor Place*

ESS-A-BAGEL (147 F4) (*ᗰ F12*)
A vast selection of bagels and an even bigger selection of cream cheese. *324th 1st Av./19th Street | tel. 1212 2 60 22 52 | www. ess-a-bagel.com | subway: L 1 Av.*

GREAT NORDIC FOOD HALL
(152 A6) (*ᗰ F9*)
New Nordic cuisine – have you tried it? In the beautiful Vanderbilt Hall of Grand Central Terminal with its huge chandeliers and walls of pink marble, you browse at various stands to test smørrebrød, pickled herring and pastries. *Mon–Fri 7am–8pm, Sat/Sun 8am–7pm | 89 E 42nd Street/ Grand Central Terminal | tel. 1646 5 68 40 20 | greatnorthernfood.com | subway: 4, 5, 6 Grand Central Terminal*

GREAT N.Y. NOODLE TOWN
(143 D3) (*ᗰ D16*)
Chinatown is bursting at the seams, with an eatery on every corner. In this busy place on Bowery you share the tables with a lot of Chinese – always a good sign! The portions are large and inexpensive. *Daily from 9am | 28 Bowery/Bayard St. | tel. 1212 3 49 09 23 | greatnynoodletown. com | subway: F East Broadway*

KIEN TUONG (143 E3) (*ᗰ D15*)
Close your eyes and enjoy at a low price: delicious roast pork with rice costs a mere $4.50 at this Vietnamese restaurant in Chinatown. Just ignore the old décor and fittings. *83 Chrystie Street/near Grand St. | tel. 1212 9 66 28 78 | subway: B, D Grand Street*

LORELEY (143 E2) (⬚ *D14*)

The imported beers are what make this German beer garden, run by renowned DJ Michael Momm, such a popular choice. *Daily | 7 Rivington Street/between Bowery and Chrystie Street | tel. 1212 25 37077 | www.loreleynyc.com | subway: F, M 2 Av.*

PORCHETTA ♲ (147 E–F6) (⬚ *E13*)

A small snack bar for everyone who likes hearty sandwiches filled with organic meat. See the website for the recipe for their brilliantly spiced roast pork. *110 E 7th Street | tel. 12127772151 | www.porchettanyc.com | subway: N, Q, 6 Astor Place/8 Street-NYU*

PRETZEL (144 A2) (⬚ *F14*)

Charming, authentic little bakery selling pretzels with cheese and ham and a whole range of sauces. *29th Av. B/3rd*

LOW BUDGET

The wine store *Chelsea Wine Vault* **(146 B3)** (⬚ *C10*) offers free wine tasting *(mostly Wed, Thu from 4pm | 75 9th Av. | tel. 1212 4 62 42 44 | www. chelseawinevault.com | subway: A, C, E 14 Street*

For a free introduction to the art of beer brewing take the ● *Brooklyn Brewery Tour* **(145 D2)** (⬚ *J14*) *(Sat, 1pm–5pm, Sun 1pm–4pm | 79 North 11th Street | tel. 1718 4 86 74 22 | www.brooklynbrewery.com | subway: L Bedford Av.)*

Eating lunch instead of dinner at one of New York's stylish restaurants e.g. sushi at *Nobu (see p. 64)* can be a money saver.

Street | tel. 1 646 410 03 33 | www.sigmundnyc.com | subway: F 2 Av.

INSIDER TIP ► SCHNITZEL & THINGS

This popular mobile food truck with its mustard coloured logo parks in a different New York street every day! For its sumptuous deep-fried cod, chicken and pork chops track it down at *www.schnitzelandthings.com* or on twitter. *Mon–Fri 11:30am to 2pm | tel. 13477727341*

SHABU-TATSU (147 E6) (⬚ *E13*)

Are you feeling shabu shabu? Then fry paper-thin slices of top-class beef fillet from Japan yourself at this fondue joint. *216 E 10th Street | tel. 1212 4 77 29 72 | www.shabutatsu.com | subway: 6 Astor Place*

SHAKE SHACK (147 E3) (⬚ *E11*)

The organic burgers here taste heavenly, even the vegetarian versions. And the French fries are magnifique! 13 branches in Manhattan and Brooklyn, e.g. in *Madison Square Park/near 23rd St. and Madison Av. | daily from 11am | tel. 1212 8 89 66 00 | www.shakeshack.com | subway: 6 23rd Street*

SILVER RICE (159 D4) (⬚ *0*)

Yes, even food from paper cups can be addictive, if they are filled with sticky rice, linseed, raw tuna or salmon tatar, slices of avocado, strips of cucumber and spicy mayonnaise. All of which tastes much better eaten outdoors. *Mon–Fri from 5pm, Sat/Sun from noon | 638 Park Place | Brooklyn | tel. 1718 3 98 82 00 | www.silverrice.com | subway: 2, 3, 4, 5 Franklin Avenue*

SMORGASBURG

At this open-air fleamarket for foodies, munch your way through the stalls selling sandwiches, chicken in buttermilk,

Craft beer ferments in the vats: the Brooklyn Brewery.

home-pickled gherkins and homemade ice cream. *April–Nov., Sat: E River State Park/Kent Av. and N 7th St. | Williamsburg | subway: L Bedford Avenue* (145 D2) *(øʄ J14); Sun: Prospect Park | Breeze Hill | Brooklyn | subway: L Bedford Avenue)* (159 D4) *(øʄ 0) | www.smorgasburg.com*

SUPERIORITY BURGER ★
(147 F6) *(øʄ E13)*

Don't be afraid of a "Sloppy Dave" – it wants to please you, just like "sneaky avocado" and "shaken tofu skin". Just go into this little stall and try the vegetarian burgers and other imaginative treats. *Thu closed | 430 E 9th Street/near First Av. | tel. 1212 2 56 11 92 | www.superiorityburger.com | subway: L First Avenue*

SYLVIA'S RESTAURANT (159 D2) *(øʄ 0)*
A popular breakfast stop in Harlem that serves traditional southern soul food. *328 Lenox Av. | tel. 1212 9 96 06 60 | www.sylviasrestaurant.com | subway: 2, 3 125 Street*

TAI THAI (144 E–F1) *(øʄ E14)*
Authentic Thai food almost at Bangkok prices! *78 E 1st Street | tel. 1212 7 77 25 52 | subway: F 2 Av.*

UMA TEMAKERIA (146 C4) *(øʄ C11)*
Mexican sushi? Here you prepare your own *temakis* (hand-made conical rolls) or seaweed burritos, all in the name of the Indian goddess Uma. New York is far out! *Daily 11am | 64 7th Av./between 14th and 15th St. | tel. 1646 3 60 32 60 | www.umatemakeria.com | subway: 1, 2, 3 14th Street*

INSIDER TIP VANESSA'S DUMPLING HOUSE

Four fried Chinese dumplings with a pork filling for $1.25, sesame pancakes with duck $3 – can it get any cheaper? *118A Eldridge Street* (143 E2) *(øʄ D–E15): tel. 1212 6 25 80 08 | subway: B, D Grant Street*; branch: *220 E 14th Street* (147 E5) *(øʄ E12): tel. 1212 5 29 13 29 | subway: L, N, Q, R, 4, 5, 6 14 Street-Union Square | www.vanessas*

SHOPPING

CITY **WHERE TO START?**
Macy's (147 E1) *(⌂ E9)*: the world's largest department store – is where you should start your New York shopping spree! This emporium takes up an entire block. And here in Herald Square you can find many more stores like H&M and Gap. For high-end boutiques head straight to **Madison Avenue** in Midtown or go directly to the Upper East Side **(152 A–B 3–5)** *(⌂ G–H 6–7)*. For bargain hunting **Broadway** in the vicinity of Houston Street **(143 D1)** *(⌂ D14)* is probably your best bet.

When flying home, you are now only allowed one suitcase of 23 kg/50.7 lbs. But there are so many things to cram into it: The list of bargains ranges from trainers to electronic devices.

There is always an excuse for the many sales you will come across in the Big Apple, be it Independence Day, Labor Day or simply clearance sales. Even books, CDs DVDs and Blu-rays are worth bargain hunting for, just be sure that the DVD country code coincides with your code back home. For some, a shopping trip in itself warrants a trip to New York. Madison and Fifth Avenue is where you will find rows of prestigious international and American designers – from Calvin Klein to Ralph Lauren – as well as high-end department stores.

The hottest trends, the latest craze, the coolest shops – New York has it all. This metropolis is a shoppers' paradise

First came SoHo and then Chelsea, then hot on their heels the *Meatpacking District* (146 B–C 3–4) *(𝄞 B–C 10–11)* – Manhattan neighbourhoods that have undergone a transformation from shabby to chic. Districts like the *Lower East Side* (143 D–F 2–4) *(𝄞 D–F 15–16)* and *Park Slope* (140 A–B 5–6) *(𝄞 k–l 23–25)* in Brooklyn are fast following suit. In the Manhattan neighbourhood of *NoLIta* (143 D1–2) *(𝄞 D–E 14–15)*, acronym for *No*rth of *Li*ttle *Ita*ly, a new genera-tion of yuppies has moved into the maze of Spring, Mott and Elizabeth Street. On the Lower East Side, *LuSTO* (143 E–F 2–3) *(𝄞 E–F 15–16)* comprising *Lu*dlow, *Stan*-ton and *O*rchard Streets, young design-ers are beginning to move into a neigh-bourhood that was once dominated by the Jewish *shmatte* (clothing) trade. Brooklyn is undergoing similar chang-es with Bedford Avenue in Williamsburg teeming with kooky little shops. The neighbourhoods on the *F Trains (Sub-*

Return to the analogue world: the Strand Book Store is a beacon of books in the digital age

way: Bergen Street or Carroll Gardens) – Boerum Hill, Cobble Hills and Carroll Gardens collectively known as BoCoCa (139 D–F 4–5) (*ill* h–k 23–22) – have design, fashion boutiques, cafés and bars. It is worth noting that the price tags in stores generally only show the net price. For food items, newspapers and books and for clothes and shoes costing less than $110, an extra 8.875 per cent in sales tax will be added on. Many stores are open on a Sunday, the long Saturday is a permanent fixture. Most shops stay open until 9pm. Opening times are only provided in this chapter when they deviate from the general rule.

BOOKS

BARNES & NOBLE

A well-known chain with outlets spread across the city. Some New Yorkers will while away an entire day here so it hardly comes as a surprise that these bookstores have become meeting places for book-loving singles. *e.g. 33 E 17th Street* (147 E4) (*ill* E12) | *subway: L, N, Q, R, 4–6 14 Street-Union Square; 97 Warren Street/ Greenwich Street* (142 B3) (*ill* B16) | *subway: 1, 2, 3 Chambers Street*

DASHWOOD BOOKS (147 D6) (*ill* D14)

Photographic books in all sizes and price categories! Go down the few steps to this magical bookshop, and you will be delighted by the small but exquisite range. *Daily from noon | 33 Bond Street | www. dashwoodbooks.com | subway: 6 Bleecker Street*

INSIDER TIP POWERHOUSE ARENA (143 E6) (*ill* E18)

A good place to go to for photography books. The shop belongs to the prestigious publishing house and sometimes it holds hip-hop parties and photo exhibitions in Dumbo, a cool area of Brooklyn. *28 Adams Street | www.powerhouse*

arena.com | subway: F York Street, A, C High Street

STRAND BOOK STORE ★ ●
(147 D–E5) (*ΩΩ E12*)

This place is quite remarkable. It has an unrivalled 18.5 miles of shelving stocked with new and used books as well as New York's largest selection of rare art and photography editions. This family business was founded in 1927 and is the sole survivor among the 47 other competitors that started out with it on New York's famous Book Row. *828 Broadway/12th Street | www.strandbooks.com | subway: L, N, Q, R, 4–6 14 Street-Union Square*

CHILDREN'S FASHION

BABY GAP (152 A4–5) (*ΩΩ G7*)

One of Gap's many Manhattan stores. It shines with unusual clothing dedicated to children from newborn to toddlers. *60 W 34th Street/6th Av. | www.gap.com | subway: B, D, F, N, Q, R 34 Street-Herald Square*

DELICATESSEN

CHELSEA MARKET ● ⊗
(146 B3) (*ΩΩ C11*)

Where the famous Oreo cookie was created, today you will find stylish shops and gourmet restaurants selling all kinds of organic and fair-trade culinary delights from across the world (from Italy and Japan to Thailand, Australia, Mexico and Morocco). The building, which once belonged to the National Biscuit Company, lends the market, including its gourmet stalls, the right kind of factory-brick charm. *75 9th Av./15th Street | subway: A, C, E 14 Street*

DEAN & DELUCA ● ⊗ (143 D1) (*ΩΩ D14*)

Gourmet deli whose espresso bar is the meeting place for New York's chic in-crowd. You can also buy culinary delights,

organically grown foods and kitchen equipment. *560 Broadway/Prince Street | www.deandeluca.com | subway: R Prince Street*

INSIDER TIP ▶ DI PALO (143 E2) (*ΩΩ D15*)

There are Italian delicacies everywhere you look in this delightful Italian deli with prosciuttos hanging from the ceiling and huge wheels of Parmesan displayed on the counter along with salamis and mozzarella. A feast for the senses. *200 Grand Street | www.dipaloselects.com | subway: B, D, Grand Street, 6 Spring Street*

MAST BROTHERS CHOCOLATE
(145 D2) (*ΩΩ J15*)

Watch as cacao beans become gourmet chocolate in Brooklyn and buy yourself a treat! *Sat/Sun noon–8pm | 111 N 3rd Street | www.mastbrothers.com | subway: L Bedford Avenue*

MARCO POLO HIGHLIGHTS

★ **Strand Book Store**
An endless selection of discounted books: paradise for (art) book lovers → p. 75

★ **Barneys New York**
Where New York's in-crowd and trendsetters meet and shop → p. 76

★ **MoMA Design Store**
Modern art and design mementos to take home → p. 80

★ **Apple Store**
The source for trendy technical gadgets → p. 76

★ **Muji**
Japanese design: purist and cool → p. 81

DEPARTMENT STORES

BARNEYS NEW YORK ⭐
(152 B4) (𝓜 G6)
Loved by the in-crowd both as a meeting place – especially at *Fred's,* a restaurant on the ninth floor – and a rather expensive place to buy their trendy clothes. The range of luxury shoes, clothes and jewellery is endless. In the building alongside it, five floors are devoted exclusively to menswear. *660 Madison Av./61st Street | www.barneys.com | subway: 4–6 59 Street*

LOW BUDGET

The gay bookstore *BGSQD* **(147 C4)** *(𝓜 C11) (Tue–Sun 1pm–7pm, during events until 9pm | 208 W 13th Street | The Community Center, Room 210 | www.bgsqd.com | subway: 1, 2, 3, 14 Street)* does not charge any fees for readings, films and festivals, but a small donation is welcome.

Designer clothing at very low prices can be found at *Century 21* **(142 B4)** *(𝓜 B17)*. *22 Cortlandt Street/between Broadway and Church Street | www.c21stores.com | subway: N, R, 1 Cortlandt Street*

● *Housing Works Bookstore Café* **(143 D1)** *(𝓜 D14) (26 Crosby Street/Houston Street | www.housingworks. org/bookstore | subway: B, D, F, M Broadway-Lafayette)* is a charming bookstore reminiscent of an old library with its winding staircase. Inexpensive books – mostly second-hand – and a quiet café with snacks and readings.

BERGDORF GOODMAN
(152 A4) (𝓜 G7)
Exclusive French, Italian and young American designers and what has to be the most attractive cosmetics department in New York. The women's store on the other side of Fifth Avenue also has a restaurant. The best Christmas window decorations in Manhattan! *754 5th Av./between 57th and 58th Street | www.bergdorfgoodman.com | subway: N, R 5 Av.*

BLOOMINGDALE'S (152 B4) (𝓜 H7)
A high-class department store selling fashion by American designers and international labels. *1000 3rd Av./between 59th and 60th Street | www.bloomingdales. com | subway: N, R, 4–6 Lexington Av./ 59 Street*

MACY'S ● (147 E1) (𝓜 E9)
The world's largest department store! Women can start their shopping spree with a make-up session downstairs before exploring its many floors for any item the heart desires. *151 W 34th Street/Broadway | www.macys.com | subway: B, D, F, N, Q , R 34 Street-Herald Square*

INSIDER TIP SUNRISE MART
(141 E6) (𝓜 E13)
The lift to Sunrise Mart is in the East Village. On the first floor is a supermarket whose beautifully packaged confectionery and odds and ends decorated with Japanese letters make ideal exotic gifts. New York's best Japanese food emporium! *Stuyvesant Street/1st floor | subway: 6 Astor Place*

ELECTRONICS

APPLE STORE ⭐ (143 D1) (𝓜 G7)
Be it the MacBook, the iPhone, the iPad or MacBook Air – Apple remains a design trendsetter. Workshops run by experts are

held daily. The biggest store in Manhattan is open around the clock. *767 5th Av./ 59th Street | www.apple.com/retail/ fifthavenue | subway: 4–6 59 Street, F 57 Street*

B+H PHOTO (147 D1) (𝄞 D9)
A shopping must for anyone with a passion for photography and film. *Mon–Thu 9am–7pm, Fri 9am–1pm, Sun 10am– 6pm | 420 9th Av./33rd Street | www.bh photovideo.com | subway: A, C, E 34 Street*

NINTENDO WORLD (151 E5) (𝄞 F8)
Game crazy? Be it Wii or Game Boy – you can try them all on more than 50 consoles. *10 Rockefeller Plaza/48th Street, 5th Av. | www.nintendoworldstore.com | subway: N, Q, R, S, 1, 2, 3, 7 Times Sq-42 Street*

FASHION & ACCESSORIES

AEROPOSTALE (147 E6) (𝄞 E9)
A chain that sells hip clothing at unbeatable prices. Young, fresh and cute fashion for girls 'n' guys. Lots of special deals. *100 W 33rd Street (147 E6) (𝄞 E9) 100 W 33rd Street | corner 6th Av. | subway: B, D, F, M, N, Q, R 34 Street | www.aeropostale.com*

AMERICAN APPAREL ⊘
(146 C5) (𝄞 D9)
These T-Shirts are not only produced in LA on the West Coast but also have the LA feel: casual understatement coupled with social commitment (no sweatshops). Many outlets. *Among others 345 7th Av./29th Street | www.americanapparel. net | subway: 1 28 Street*

INSIDER TIP BEACON'S CLOSET
Four women from Brooklyn got their heads together, and the result was this chain of cool stores for vintage clothes. Classic, off-the-wall and, as *Time Out*

wrote, a "killer shoe selection"! Four addresses, e.g.: *10 W 13th Street (147 D4) (𝄞 E12) Manhattan | subway: F, M 14 Street; 74 Guernsey St. (159 D3) (𝄞 O) Brooklyn | subway: G Nassau Avenue | www.beaconscloset.com*

Shopping galore at Macy's, the world's largest department store

BROOKLYN INDUSTRIES
Bags, cool T-shirts, jackets, clothes in Brooklyn style. *290 Lafayette Street (143 D1) (𝄞 D14) subway: B, D, F, M Broadway-Lafayette; branch: 500 Hudson Street (146 B5) (𝄞 B12) subway: 1 Christopher Street | www.brooklyn industries.com*

DARLING (146 C4) (𝄞 C11)
Unconventional, charming, sexy and very affordable best describes Ann French

Emonts' fashion designs. Aside from her own creations she also carries fashions by other New York design talents. WiFi in the garden. *1 Horatio Street/8th Av. | www. darlingnyc.com | subway: A, C, E, L 14 Street*

LIQUOR STORE (142 C2) (*∅ B15*)

What was once a bar now houses the J. Crew's menswear boutique. The Steve McQueen-look is cultivated here. *235 W Broadway | www.jcrew.com | subway: A, C, E 1 Canal Street*

MARC JACOBS (143 D1) (*∅ D14*)

His and her fashion and accessories by the crown prince of American designers. *113 Prince Street/between Green and Wooster | www.marcjacobs.com | subway: N, R Prince Street*

PRADA (143 D1) (*∅ D14*)

The Prada store offers a very 21st-century shopping experience – its changing rooms have some very high-tech features. *575 Broadway/Prince Street |* *www.prada.com | subway: N, R Prince Street*

REI (143 D1) (*∅ D14*)

This cooperative sells everything you need for walking, skiing, climbing, canoeing, jogging or cycling, from a rucksack to a down jacket or a ski suit. The sales staff give excellent advice, and the building in SoHo is one of the most attractive in the district. *303 Lafayette Street | www.rei.com | subway: B, D, F, M Broadway-Lafayette*

TODD SNYDER (147 E3) (*∅ E10*)

Get clothed, have a shave and drink at the same time! A newly opened trendy shop for menswear (shoes, jeans, coats and glasses) INSIDER TIP with a bar and barbershop. *25 E 26th Street | www. toddsnyder.com | subway: N, R 23 Street*

TOPSHOP/TOPMAN (151 E5) (*∅ F8*)

Elegant clothing in the flagship store of the famous British chain. *608 5th Av./*

O holy glass cube: disciples of technology outside New York's Apple Store

49th Street | www.topshop.com | subway: B, D, F, M, 47–50 St.-Rockefeller Center

URBAN OUTFITTERS
(151 E6) (*m F8*)

This store has piles of cool clothes plus records and a small café on the first floor. Not cheap, but novel and hip. *521 5th Av./43rd Street | www.urbanout fitters.com | subway: 4–7, S Grand Central-42 Street*

VIVIENNE WESTWOOD
(151 F4) (*m G7*)

London punk velvet for men and women on three floors by the red-haired fashion icon Vivienne Westwood. How about a heart-shaped black leather bag? It's yours for $400! *14 E 55 Street | www.viviennewestwood.com | subway: E, M 5 Avenue/53 Street*

FLEA MARKETS

In New York Sunday is the day for flea markets, street fairs and crafts fairs. More information in the city magazines.

ARTISTS & FLEAS

Local artists, designers and crafts-people sell jewellery, clothes and much more at the weekend in a warehouse at *70 North 7th Street* (145 D2) (*m J15*) *(between Kent and Wythe Av. | Williamsburg | subway: L Bedford Avenue* or at the *Chelsea Market* (see p. 75) *(daily | 88 10th Av./15th Street | subway: A, C, E 14 Street). www.artistsand fleas.com*

GALLERIES

Opening hours generally 10am–6pm, often closed Sun/Mon. On Thursdays many have an exhibition opening from 6pm.

DAVID ZWIRNER (146 B2) (*m B10*)

Exhibits influential artists like Neo Rauch and Marcel Dzamas and fosters the careers of future stars. Elegant house with garden. *537 W 20th Street/between 10th and 11th Av. | www.davidzwirner.com | subway: C, E 23 Street*

INSIDER TIP KINFOLK STUDIOS
(145 D2) (*m J14*)

An experimental mix of gallery, bar and designer's studio has opened its doors in trendy Williamsburg. Check it out! *90 Wythe Av. | Brooklyn | www.kinfolk studios.com | subway: L Bedford Av.*

JEWELLERY

TIFFANY & CO. (152 A4) (*m G7*)

The legendary New York jewellery store that has prices that are equally legendary! Head to the third floor for affordable silver knick-knacks. *727 5th Av./57th Street | www.tiffany.com | subway: B, C 57 Street*

MALL

WOODBURY COMMON PREMIUM OUTLETS (0) (*m 0*)

Located outside the city, it is a popular attraction with its 220 outlet stores from world famous high-end brands like Prada, Miu Miu, Marc Jacobs, Armani and Gucci. *Take the Short Line bus from Port Authority (second floor) | fare of $42 includes discount vouchers | www. premiumoutlets.com*

MISCELLANEOUS

INSIDER TIP AJI ICHIBAN
(143 D3) (*m D15*)

Japanese confectionery and savoury snacks in Chinatown – colourful small bowls laid out so you can try before you buy. *137 Mott | subway: 6 Canal Street*

BEADS OF PARADISE (147 D4) (*☐ D11*)

Smiling Buddhas in yellow, green and red, display cases bursting with jewellery, silk scarves and beads galore for creative buyers. Just make your New York jewellery yourself! *16 E 17th Street/5th Av. | www. beadsofparadisenyc.com | subway: L, N, Q, R, 4–6 14 Street-Union Square*

HAMMACHER SCHLEMMER (152 B4) (*☐ H7*)

An eclectic mix of gifts ranging from a hi-tech futuristic noise neutraliser to your traditional pair of slippers. *Closed Sun | 147 E 57th Street | near Lexington Av. | www. hammacher.com | subway: N, R, 4–6 Lexington Av./59 Street*

British fashion in the Big Apple: no problem at all at Topshop

CONTAINER STORE (147 D3) (*☐ D11*)

Packaging, storage, filing – every conceivable box, container or chest in any conceivable colour and shape for kitchen, office or garage use or a gift as well as everything for traveling is sold here. *629 6th Av. | www.containerstore.com | subway: F, M 23 Street*

FISH'S EDDY ☺ (147 E4) (*☐ E11*)

A shop that sells everything from mugs with New York motifs and plates depicting the city's skyline to T-Shirts made from organic cotton. Ideal for souvenirs. *889 Broadway/19th Street | www.fishseddy. com | subway: R, 6 23 Street*

LOVE, ADORNED (143 E1) (*☐ D14*)

Unique shop for jewellery, accessories, bits & bobs and home deco items in SoHo. *269 Elizabeth Street/E Houston Street | www.loveadorned.com | subway: F 2nd Avenue*

MAKARI (147 E5) (*☐ E13*)

Precious Japanese items, crafts and tiny antiques: a bit of Tokyo at the heart of the East Village. Quiet, elegant and not easy on the wallet – but it costs nothing to look. *97 Third Av./near 12 St. | themakari.com | subway: L 3 Avenue*

MOMA DESIGN STORE ★

A great décor selection and a whole range of items for everyday use from the collection of the Museum of Modern Art. Several branches in the city: *11 W 53rd Street* (151 E–F 4–5) *(⌕ G7)* | *between 5th and 6th Av.* | *subway: B, D, F, M 47 Street-50 Street; 81 Spring Street/Crosby Street* (143 D1) *(⌕ D14)* | *subway: 6 Spring Street* | *www.momastore.org*

MUJI ★ (142 C2) *(⌕ C15)*
Waterproof speakers, New York skyscrapers made from wooden blocks, unusual fashion – a wide variety of interesting household novelties. Four branches. *455 Broadway* | *www.muji.us* | *subway: N, Q, 6 Canal Street*

STORY (146 B2) *(⌕ B10)*
Once a month this shop changes its range of knick-knacks to cover a new subject: love, for example, wellbeing or New York. Expect to be surprised. This is a good place to buy gifts. *144 10th Av./near 19th St.* | *thisisstory.com* | *subway: C, E 23 Street*

INSIDER TIP WING ON WO & CO. (143 D3) *(⌕ C16)*
The oldest shop in Chinatown (founded in 1890!) has charm and antique porcelain: porcelain figures, glazed bowls, colourful cups or even a whole tea set. Three generations of a Chinese family have run this store. *26 Mott Street* | *www.wingonwoand.co* | *subway: J, Z Chambers Street*

MUSIC

ACADEMY RECORDS (149 D6) *(⌕ J13)*
Vinyl is alive – and kicking! This impressive record store in Greenpoint/ Brooklyn has more than 100,000 new and secondhand discs in stock. As well as CDs. *85 Oak Street/between W St. and Franklin St.* | *www.academy-lps.com* | *subway: G Greenpoint Avenue*

JAZZ RECORD CENTER (147 D2) *(⌕ D10)*
The name says it all – jazz is what this store is all about. *Closed Sun* | *236 W 26th Street/between 7th and 8th Av., 8th floor* | *www.jazzrecordcenter.com* | *subway: 1 28 Street*

SALONS & COSMETICS

AVEDA INSTITUTE (142 C1) *(⌕ C 14)*
A beauty salon ideal for a quick treatment in between shopping. The institute is also a school so if you let trainees do your facial or colour, it could cost half of what you would normally pay and the trainees tend to be twice as careful! *233 Spring Street/between 6th Av. and Varick Street* | *tel. 1 212 807 14 92* | *www.avedainstitute ny.com* | *subway: 1 Houston Street*

FRÉDÉRIC FEKKAI (152 A4) *(⌕ G7)*
Stylist to the stars, his clients included celebrities like Liv Tyler and Naomi Watts. Today, he himself doesn't do haircuts anymore, but still they don't come cheap – a cut can cost you between $135 and $275 if it is by a creative director. *712 5th Av./56th Street* | *tel. 1 212 7 53 95 00* | *www.fekkai.com* | *subway: E, F 5 Av.*

KIEHL'S PHARMACY ☺ (147 E5) *(⌕ E12)*
Beautiful old-fashioned pharmacy famous for its own skin and hair care cosmetics line. No animal testing. Three outlets in New York, the most beautiful is *109 3rd Av./between 13th and 14th Street* | *www.kiehls.com* | *subway: L, N, Q, R, 4–6 14 Street-Union Square*

SEPHORA (143 D1) *(⌕ D14)*
This is where New York's glamour crowd go for their beauty tips. *555 Broadway/between Houston and Prince Street* | *www.sephora.com* | *subway: N, R Prince Street*

ENTERTAINMENT

CITY WHERE TO START?
New York's nightlife is as varied as the city itself. A musical in the Theater District? Greenwich Village for some live jazz? Or one of the many smaller bars and live music clubs in the Lower East Side? The world is your oyster here and what better way to kick off your evening than at **Salon de Ning (152 A4)** *(☉ G7)* on the rooftop of The Peninsula hotel. From here the city sparkles seductively. After a drink, plunge into the nightlife of the Big Apple.

In the entertainment capital of the world New Yorkers seldom head home right after work but prefer to meet for drinks in their favourite bar and then move on to an early dinner at the city's newest hot spot.

Straight afterwards, they head to the theatre, the opera, a musical or the movies, ending the evening on a high note at one of the city's hip and trendy clubs. While visitors can feel quite overwhelmed, New Yorkers themselves are almost blasé about being spoilt for choice – they know what they like and often check out what the newspaper critics have to say. The clubs especially rely

The Big Apple knows exactly how to lay it on with a limitless choice of musicals, theatre, jazz, opera, bars, discos and nightclubs

on what is in and their popularity is constantly in the throes of change. One thing is certain though, live music will always stand its ground in the Big Apple, especially jazz, blues and rock. Many night owls are now drawn to the hipster neighbourhoods of Williamsburg and Bushwick in Brooklyn – the prices here are lower, but the music and the locations are cooler.

BARS

Hotel bars are a popular meeting place for New Yorkers who gather there till late at night enjoying traditional New York cocktails such as Martinis, Manhattans, Gimlets or Whisky Sours. Hot spots are the *King Cole Bar* in *The Street Regis*, the ♨ *Le Bain* on the *Standard* and the *Grand Bar* in the *Hotel Soho Grand*.

New York is cocktail crazy! Drinks from the 17th and 18th centuries are now all the rage. Popular ones include the "Bishop", a kind of mulled wine (red wine with anise, clove and orange), the "Flip" (high-proof alcohol with egg and sugar) and the "Cobbler" (wine, fruit and sugar). These mixed drinks may be full of creativ-

4 22 71 03 | www.abcbeer.co | subway: F 2nd Avenue

INSIDER TIP▶ APOTHÉKE (143 D3) (*DD D16*)
Here you will be served blazing shots of absinthe by barmen wearing white pharmacists' coats. The green liquid was prohibited for many years – now it is all the

Balthazar – for a taste of France in the middle of New York

ity, but they will knock you off your feet. It is important to carry some form of ID even if you clearly are 21 years or older – the minimum age at which you may order alcohol in the United States – as bars often request them before serving clients.

230 FIFTH ☼ (147 E2) (*DD E10*)
This large, award-winning roof terrace bar on Fifth Avenue lies at the heart of Midtown's sea of lights. *230 5th Av./27th Street | tel. 1212 7 25 43 00 | www.230-fifth.com | subway: N, R, 6 28 Street*

ALPHABET CITY BEER CO.
(144 A1) (*DD F14*)
Voted New York's best bar in 2016! In the hip East Village, locals recline on a leather sofa to drink one of over 350 kinds of beer. How about a Boulevard Funky Pumpkin? *96 Av. C/near 7th St. | tel. 1646*

rage and this bar is packed every evening. *9 Doyers Street/between The Bowery and Pell Street | tel. 1212 4 06 04 00 | apothek enyc.com | subway: N, Q, 6 Canal Street*

BALTHAZAR (143 D1) (*DD D14*)
Trendy without being ostentatious this French brasserie is perfect for celebrity spotting from the bar. The steak frites are in great demand. *80 Spring Street/Crosby Street | tel. 1212 9 65 14 14 | www.balthazar ny.com | subway: 6 Spring Street*

INSIDER TIP▶ BARCADE
Two bars styled as game arcades where you can play legendary video games from the 1980s for 25 cents. A freshly poured beer rounds off the retro fun. *Manhattan: 148 W 24th Street (147 D2) (DD D10) (tel. 1212 3 90 84 55 | www.barcadenewyork. com | subway: 1, 23 Street); Brooklyn:*

388 Union Av. (145 E4) *(K16)* *(tel. 1718 3 02 64 64 | www.barcadebrooklyn.com | subway: L Lorimer Street)*

BATHTUB GIN (146 C3) *(C10)*
The name alludes to gin that was made in the bathtub during Prohibition. Charming place with cocktails and snacks. *132 9th Av./between 18th and 19th Street | tel. 1646 5 59 16 71 | www.bathtubginnyc.com | subway: A, C, E 14 Street*

BEMELMAN'S BAR (152 C2) *(H5)*
The stylish interior of this romantic piano bar in the Carlyle Hotel attracts a chic and elegant clientele. *35 E 76th Street/ Madison Av. | tel. 1212 7 44 16 00 | subway: 6 77 Street*

INSIDER TIP **THE BLIND BARBER**
(147 F6) *(F13)*
Have your hair cut in this nostalgic, old-school barber shop in East Village for only $45 or your beard trimmed for $50 and enjoy a cocktail included in the price. *339 E 10th Street | tel. 1212 228 21 23 | blindbarber.com | subway: L 1 Av.*

BRASS MONKEY (146 B3) *(B11)*
This bar has a relaxed atmosphere unlike most of the otherwise crowded places in the Meatpacking District. View of the Hudson River from the rooftop terrace. *55 Little W 12th Street/between Washington Street and 10th Av. | tel. 1212 6 75 66 86 | brassmonkeynyc.com | subway: A, C, E, 14 Street*

BRASSERIE 8½ (152 A4) *(G7)*
Its lively bar scene and retro décor makes this a Midtown hot spot for New York's in-crowd. *9 W 57th Street/between 5th and 6th Av. | tel. 1212 8 29 08 12 | www.brasserie812.com | subway: B, Q 6 Av.*

CIBAR LOUNGE (147 E4) *(E12)*
Amazing Martini selection which you can enjoy in front of the fireplace in the bamboo garden! *56 Irving Place/between 17th and 18th Street | tel. 1212 4 60 56 56 |*

MARCO POLO HIGHLIGHTS

★ **Salon de Ning**
Get a view of New York's skyscrapers by night when you have a drink on the rooftop terrace → p. 87

★ **Broadway musicals**
In New York? A must-see for every visitor → p. 88

★ **Le Poisson Rouge**
Said to have the city's best nightclub music → p. 90

★ **Dizzy's Club Coca Cola**
This club in the Lincoln Center is a jazz classic → p. 91

★ **David Geffen Hall**
Home to the New York Philharmonic Orchestra → p. 93

★ **City Center**
Captivating ballet performances in a restored theatre → p. 94

★ **Metropolitan Opera**
Only the most famous opera stars in the world get to perform on this stage → p. 94

★ **Brooklyn Academy of Music**
Dance, music, drama, film, literature, comedy ... an adventurous cultural whirlwind → p. 95

BARS

www.cibarlounge.com | subway: N, Q, R, 4–6 14 Street–Union Square

THE DEAD RABBIT GROCERY AND GROG (142 B6) (𝄡 B18)
This bar was named after an infamous 19th-century gang. Drinks are mixed vigorously on two floors: punch, bishops, flips and cobblers are on offer. *30 Water Street | tel. 1 646 4 22 79 06 | www. deadrabbitnyc.com | subway: N, R Whitehall Street*

THE DELANCEY (143 F2) (𝄡 E15)
The roof not only has a bar, but also a garden with a fish pond and a dance club. Don't miss it!. *168 Delancey Street | tel. 1 212 2 54 99 20 | www.thedelancey. com | subway: F Delancey Street*

INSIDER TIP▶ THE FREEHOLD
(144 C3) (𝄡 H16)
This seriously trendy hotel bar in Williamsburg has no hotel, but drinks indoors and outdoors, ping-pong tables, WiFi and lots of people from the neighbourhood. *45 S 3rd Street/near Wythe Av. | tel. 1 718 3 88 75 91 | www. freeholdbrooklyn.com | subway: J, M, Z Marcey Avenue*

HENRY PUBLIC (139 D3) (𝄡 H21)
Cosy and sophisticated: this old-fashioned bar looks like an elegant British pub from the 19th century. Look forward to classic long drinks, creative cocktails and delicious bites like the organic burger or the turkey sandwich, which won an award from *New York Magazine. 329 Henry Street/near Atlantic Av. | tel. 1 718 8 52 86 30 | www.henrypublic. com | subway: 2, 3, 4, 5 Borough Hall*

HOUSE OF WAX (139 F3) (𝄡 K21)
This place is macabre. More than 100 anatomical models, a collection brought from Berlin, are displayed around the counter: wax models that show parts of the body, surgical operations and abnormalities. The drink to match is a Napoleon Death Mask. *445 Albee Square W | 4th floor | Brooklyn | tel. 1 929 3 82 54 03 | www.thehouseofwax.com | subway: 2, 3 Hoyt Street*

LOUNGE AT POD 39 HOTEL ☄
(148 A1) (𝄡 G9)
The rooftop terrace with a spectacular view of the Empire State Building has a Spanish flair thanks to its brick arches. *145 E 39th Street | tel. 1 212 8 65 57 00 | www.thepodhotel.com | subway: 4–7, S Grand Central-42 Street*

MCSORLEY'S OLD ALE HOUSE
(147 E6) (𝄡 E13)
New York's oldest bar was a men-only bar right up to 1970. The floor is covered in sawdust and drinks are limited to a choice of *light* and *dark beer* and you have to order two drinks at a time. *15 E 7th Street/ 3rd Av. | tel. 1 212 473 91 48 | mcsorley soldalehouse.nyc | subway: 6 Astor Place*

THE NOMAD BAR
(147 E2) (𝄡 E10)
Ladies and gentlemen, this luxurious bar has won the grand prix for the most elegant and coolest bar in Manhattan. Some think it is the best in the world, but Americans always exaggerate. Sip an Espresso Spiked Manhattan and decide for yourself. *10 W 28th Street | tel. 1 212 7 96 15 00 | www.thenomadhotel.com | subway: N, R 28th Street*

PEGU CLUB (143 D1) (𝄡 D14)
According to *New York Magazine*, here Audrey Saunders mixes the best Martini – "shockingly strong". The bar is romantic, too, named after an officers' club in 19th-century Burma. *77 W Hous-*

A warm summer evening up high on the terrace of the Press Lounge

ton Street | tel. 1212 473 73 48 | www.peguclub.com | subway: C, E Spring Street

PRAVDA (143 D1) *(⌂ D14)*
The rosemary Martini served in the cocktail lounge in SoHo is an absolute must! *281 Lafayette Street/Prince Street | tel. 1212 226 49 44 | www.pravdany.com | subway: N, R Prince Street*

PRESS LOUNGE ● ⌒ (150 C4) *(⌂ D6)*
Ink48's spacious hotel rooftop bar around the pool with brilliant views. *653 11 Av./48th Street | tel. 1212 757 22 24 | www.ink48.com | subway: C, E, 1 50 Street*

INSIDERTIP ▶ ROYAL PALM SHUFFLE
(139 F5) *(⌂ J23)*
A shuffleboard club in Brooklyn where a board costs $40 per hour, games for two or four. Drink to the finish at the bar. *514 Union Street | tel. 1347 2 23 44 10 | www.royalpalmshuffle.com | subway: R Union Street*

RUDY'S BAR (150 C5) *(⌂ E7)*
There is always something on the go in this small pub. The waitresses rush around with huge pitchers (and the free hot dogs that go with them). *627 9th Av./45th Street | tel. 1646 7 07 08 90 | www.rudysbarnyc.com | subway: A, C, E 42 Street-Port Authority Bus Terminal*

SALON DE NING ★ ⌒
(152 A4) *(⌂ G7)*
A glass enclosed terrace on the roof of the 23rd floor of *The Peninsula* hotel. In the summer you sit on the terrace between the skyscrapers and look into the sky above the city. *700 5th Av./55th Street | tel. 1212 9 56 28 88 | subway: E, M 5 Av.*

SMITH & MILLS
(142 B2) *(⌂ B15)*
This charming and offbeat pub in a restored coach house is a great place to enjoy some cocktails. *71 N Moore Street | tel. 1212 226 25 15 | www.smithandmills.com | subway: 1 Franklin Street*

TØRST (145 E1) *(⌂ K14)*
Named the best bar for beer by the magazine *Time Out*. Try Danish snacks to go with it and enjoy the Scandinavian ambience in hip Greenpoint. *615 Man-*

hattan Av./between Driggs and Nassau Av. | tel. 1 718 3 89 60 34 | www.torstnyc. com | subway: G Nassau Av.

BROADWAY & MUSICALS

There are more than 40 theatres on Broadway, almost all of them in the Theater District. ⭐ *Musicals* are the real money-spinners, with more than 13 million tickets a year sold. Count yourself extremely lucky if you get hold of tickets for the hip-hop musical "Hamilton" – it's almost impossible. A number of shows have been box office hits for many years – *The Phantom of the Opera* has been going for almost 30 years. With hit shows ranging from *The Book of Mormon* from the creators of the TV series *South Park* to Cyndi Lauper's *Kinky Books* and the Abba-based musical *Mamma Mia!,* there is something for everyone. Most theatres are closed on Mondays. There are often matinees on a Wednesday, Saturday and Sunday. Programme schedules and reviews can be found in the *New York Times (Fri and Sun),* the *New York Magazine* and *The New Yorker.*

CLUBS & POP/ROCK/SALSA

For event listings use *New York, Time Out* or the *Village Voice.* The *New Yorker* or the *New York Times* is your best bet for live music. For club information go to *www.ny.com.* Most venues will charge a *cover charge* (CC: price per person). For the best chances in getting in, dress up. Try a number of clubs as the doormen all have different tastes.

ARLENE'S GROCERY (143 F2) *(ọ E14)*
A young audience and young bands. The musicians on stage change hourly and there is lots of loud noise and high energy. *CC $5–10 | 95 Stanton Street/Orchard Street | tel. 1 212 3 58 16 33 | www. arlenes grocery.net | subway: F 2 Av.*

INSIDER TIP ▶ BARBES ● (158 C4) *(ọ 0)*
Good jazz, eastern European wind instruments, world music: the charming location, excellent live music, free entrance and an eclectic mix of patrons of all ages have elevated this small gem in Brooklyn to cult status. *376 9th Street/6th Av. | tel. 1 347 422 02 48 | www.barbesbrooklyn. com | subway: F, G 7 Av.*

INSIDER TIP ▶ THE BELL HOUSE (145 C4) *(ọ J15)*
One of the best clubs in New York with live bands, DJs, ping-pong and bingo contests and TV parties. Many events are free of charge, some cost $10 – the occasional concert will be pricier. *149 7th Street | tel. 1 718 643 65 10 | www. thebellhouseny.com | subway: F, G 9 Street-4 Av.*

BOWERY BALLROOM (143 E2) *(ọ D15)*
Hip up-and-coming indie bands and old names like Patti Smith take it in turns

ENTERTAINMENT

on the stage here. *CC $10–50 | 6 Delancey Street/between Bowery and Chrystie Street | tel. 1212 533 21 11 | www.boweryballroom.com | subway: F Delancey Street*

BOWERY ELECTRIC (147 E6) (*m D14*)
A club on the Bowery with dance DJs and live rock concerts. It covers two floors with three bars. *327 Bowery/2nd Street | tel. 1212 2 28 02 28 | theboweryelectric.com | subway: 6 Bleecker Street*

CAKE SHOP (143 F2) (*m E15*)
Indie and underground music at its best can be heard in this vaulted cellar on the Lower East Side. Aside from beers being served upstairs, you can also order coffee and cake – the cupcakes are a huge hit! *152 Ludlow Street/Stanton Street | tel. 1212 253 00 36 | www.cake-shop.com | subway: F Delancey Street*

CIELO CLUB (146 B3) (*m B11*)
World-class DJs turn the night into a party in the trendy Meatpacking District. *CC $12–25 | 18 Little W 12th Street | tel.* 1212 6 45 57 00 | www.cieloclub.com | subway: A, C, E, L 14 Street/8 Av.

INSIDER TIP GONZALES Y GONZALES (143 D1) (*m D14*)
Salsa lovers, swing your hips! From Wednesday to Sunday this is the spot for some sensual dancing (salsa, merengue, reggae sound) and Mexican eats. *192 Mercer Street | tel. 1212 4 73 78 78 | gygnyc.com | subway: 6 Bleecker Street*

INSIDER TIP HOUSE OF YES (159 D3) (*m 0*)
Have you ever done yoga to techno music? If not, then don't miss Bushwick, which is getting trendier all the time. Here in the House of Yes you see acrobatics and burlesque dancing. A colourful, crazy mix of events, restaurant, bar and garden. *2 Wykoff Av. | Brooklyn | tel. 1 585 2 17 72 09 | www.houseofyes.org | subway: L Jefferson Street*

MARQUEE (146 C1) (*m C9*)
Funky house music, hip-hop or techno remixes to get you into the groove. *CC*

A world-famous sea of lights at the heart of the entertainment world: Broadway

$20 | 289 10th Av./26th Street | tel. 1646 4 73 02 02 | www.marqueeny.com | subway: C, E 23 Street

MERCURY LOUNGE (143 F2) (*ΩΩ E14*)
Hip and exciting! Showcase for up-and-coming bands hoping to make it big. Cheap tickets! CC $10–15 | 217 E Houston Street/Essex Street | tel. 1212 2 60 47 00 | www.mercuryloungenyc.com | subway: F 2 Av.

PIANOS
(143 E–F2) (*ΩΩ E15*)
Instead of buying concert tickets, go to this bar and use the money to enjoy some drinks and excellent live music for free or for a low admission. 158 Ludlow Street | tel. 1212 5 05 37 33 | www.pianosnyc.com | subway: F 2 Av.

LOW BUDGET

Crime writers, celebrities and others read at *Barnes & Noble* (see p. 74). Flyers at the stores carry scheduled events.

The *Central Park Summer Stage* (152 B2) (*ΩΩ H5*) *(Rumsey Playfield, at 72nd Street | www.summerstage. org | subway: 6 68 Street-Hunter College)* offers free open-air concerts in July and August.

See the *Late Show with Stephen Colbert* live. Book free tickets on the day of the show right there at the Ed Sullivan Theater (151 E4) (*ΩΩ F7*) *(Mon–Thu 9:30am–noon; show: Mon–Thu 5:30pm | 1697 Broadway | www.colbert lateshow.com | subway: B, D, E 7 Av.*

LE POISSON ROUGE ⭐
(146 C6) (*ΩΩ C13*)
The club with the best music in Manhattan – from Lady Gaga to David Byrne. The concerts range from experimental and folk to classical and opera. 156 Bleecker Street | tel. 1212 5 05 34 74 | www.lepoissonrouge.com | subway: A–F, M W 4 Street

INSIDERTIP ▸ ROCKWOOD MUSIC HALL
(143 E2) (*ΩΩ E14*)
There are live concerts every evening and the band has to be small otherwise there isn't enough space for the guests. Red velvet curtains enclose this glassed-in music bar where admission is usually free, the music fantastic and the patrons friendly. 196 Allen Street/Houston Street | tel. 1212 477 41 55 | www.rockwood musichall.com | subway: F 2 Av.

INSIDERTIP ▸ ROUGH TRADE
(145 D2) (*ΩΩ J15*)
Williamsburg is home to the LP and CD shop of the Rough Trade music label. In the evening the bar and concert space are open for live music, sometimes free, sometimes for up to $25. 64 N 9th Street | tel. 1 718 3 88 41 11 | www.roughtrade. com | subway: L Bedford Avenue

S.O.B.'S (146 B6) (*ΩΩ C13*)
The name is an abbreviation for "Sounds of Brazil", so if Caribbean and Brazilian music or salsa and reggae are your thing then this is the place for you. CC $10–40 | 204 Varick Street/Houston Street | tel. 1212 2 43 49 40 | www.sobs.com | subway: 1 Houston Street

UNION HALL (158 C4) (*ΩΩ O*)
Something for everyone: downstairs karaoke, comedy, live music and DJs, upstairs play boccia, sit by the fireplace and browse in the house library. 702 Union

Street/near Fifth Av. | Brooklyn | tel. 1 718 6 38 44 00 | www.unionhallnyc.com | subway: R Union Street

INSIDER TIP ▶ WARSAW CLUB
(145 F1–2) *(ᗢ L14)*

One of the city's hot spots for rock, indie and punk! Except on Saturday when couples 40 and over come here to dance the polka. *CC from $10 | 261 Driggs Av./ Eckford Street | Brooklyn | tel. 1 718 3 87 05 05 | www.warsawconcerts.com | subway: L Lorimer Street*

JAZZ & BLUES

For jazz and blues music events refer to the Friday's *New York Times (Pop and Jazz Guide | www.nytimes.com)*.

ARTHUR'S TAVERN **(146 C5)** *(ᗢ C12)*

Live jazz and blues every evening in this slightly old-fashioned nightclub in West Village. A reason to go: it's not so crowded as some of the better-known clubs. *57 Grove Street/near Seventh Av. | tel. 1 212 6 75 68 79 | arthurstavernnyc.com | subway: 1 Christopher Street*

THE BLUE NOTE
(146 C5) *(ᗢ C13)*

This famous club with the most famous performers may be crowded and often expensive, but the music is brilliant. Reservation essential! *CC $10–75 | 131 W 3rd Street/6th Av. | tel. 1 212 4 75 85 92 | www.bluenote.net | subway: A–F, M W 4 Street*

DIZZY'S CLUB COCA COLA ★
(151 E3) *(ᗢ F6)*

The crème de la crème of jazz grooves in this club in the Lincoln Center. *CC $10–150 plus $10 minimum meal charge | 33 W 60th Street/10 Columbus Circle | at the Time Warner Center | tel.*

A tropical feeling with the music to match: it's the rhythm that matters at S.O.B.'s

1 212 2 58 95 95 | www.jazz.org | subway: A–D, 1 59 Street-Columbus Circle

KNICKERBOCKER BAR & GRILL
(147 D5) (ΩΩ D12)

A wood-panelled bar with leather chairs and absolutely outstanding pianists and bass players. *Live music Fri, Sat from 9:45pm | CC $3.50 | 33 University Place/*

Village Vanguard hits the high notes with jazz lovers

9th Street | tel. 1 212 2 28 84 90 | www. knickerbockerbarandgrill.com | subway: 6 Astor Place

KNITTING FACTORY (142 C3) (ΩΩ K16)

Avant-garde or traditional jazz, alternative rock and pop – this legendary club is also an entertainment business with its own record labels and branches around the USA. The programme runs to events like brunch with drag queens and regular comedy evenings. *CC $5–20 | 361 Metropolitan Av. | Brooklyn | tel. 1 347 5 29 66 96 | www.knittingfactory.com | subway: L Bedford Av.*

MINTON'S
(155 F1) (ΩΩ 0)

Giants like Charlie Parker, Thelonious Monk and Dizzy Gillespie played here in the 1940s. The ultimate New York jazz experience! *Live music Fri–Sun | 206 W 118 Street | tel. 1 212 2 43 22 22 | www. mintonsharlem.com | subway: B, C 116 Street*

INSIDER TIP ▶ PARLOR ENTERTAINMENT
● (159 D1) (ΩΩ 0)

Every Sunday at 4pm Marjorie Eliot, a grand old lady of the jazz piano, invites you in to her lounge in Harlem for a jazz concert. *Entrance free of charge, voluntary contribution | 555 Edgecombe Av./160th Street | Apt 3F | tel. 1 212 7 81 65 95 | subway: C 163 Street*

SMALL'S (146 C5) (ΩΩ C12)

Who said there's nothing going on in the cellar? Top-class jazz is played here in the basement until 4am – so it's often packed, but good! *CC $20 | 183 W 10th Street/7th Av. | tel. 1 212 9 29 75 65 | www.smallsjazzclub.com | subway: 1 Christopher Street*

THE VILLAGE VANGUARD
(146 C4) (ΩΩ C12)

New York's most prestigious jazz club in Greenwich Village has top-class artists and the best acoustics in town. *CC $30–40 plus one drink | 178 S 7th Av./11th Street | tel. 1 212 2 55 40 37 | www.villagevanguard.com | subway: 1–3 14 Street*

ENTERTAINMENT

CINEMA & FILM

The latest film releases often premiere in several cinemas at once. For movie listings, check out the *New York Times* and the *New York Post*, as well as the weekly magazines *New York Magazine* and *The New Yorker.*

NITEHAWK CINEMA
(145 D3) (*J16*)

If you feel hungry in this cinema in Williamsburg, you can still stay in your seat until the showdown: the menu, with burgers, beer and salads, is as long as a space cruiser in Star Wars. *136 Metropolitan Av./between Berry Street and Wythe Av. | Brooklyn | www.nitehawkcinema. com | subway: J, M, Z Marcy Avenue*

CONCERTS

New York would not be New York without its many open-air shows held here in the summer. *Mostly Mozart* and *Classical Jazz* held in the Lincoln Center courtyard are all-time favourites. The Metropolitan Opera and the philharmonic orchestra offer INSIDER TIP *concerts in parks,* four of them in Central Park. There and in Brooklyn's Prospect Park you can listen to jazz musicians, pop stars and rock bands. When the weather is good, do as the New Yorkers do: buy some goodies, arrive early and sit down on the concert lawn for a picnic. *Events schedule: Lincoln Center (tel. 1212 5 46 26 56 | www.lincoln center.org).*

BARCLAYS CENTER
(140 B4) (*I23*)

The hip-hop mogul Jay-Z supported the opening of the giant Barclays Center in Brooklyn. The Brooklyn Nets basketball team plays here as well as the heavy metal band Iron Maiden or the singer and songwriter Ed Sheeran. Almost 20,000 spectators fit into the hall. *620 Atlantic Av. | tel. 1917 6 18 61 00 | www.barclayscenter.com | subway: B, D, N, Q, R, 2, 3, 4, 5 Atlantic Av.-Barclays Center*

BARGEMUSIC ● 🎵
(143 E5) (*D18*)

A very special concert hall: Chamber music on a ship docked in Brooklyn with a great (night) view of Manhattan. *Thu–Sat 8pm, Sun 4pm | Fulton Ferry Landing | tickets $35–40 | tel. 1 718 624 20 83 | www. bargemusic.org | subway: 2, 3 Clark Street*

CARNEGIE HALL (151 E4) (*F6*)

Concerts by world-famous musicians and orchestras are held in Carnegie Hall which is often used for recordings because of its acoustics. *Backstage tours Oct–June Mon–Fri 11:30am, 12:30pm, 2pm, 3pm, Sat 11:30am and 12:30pm, Sun 12:30pm | 57th Street/7th Av. | admission $17 | tel. 1 212 9 03 97 65 | www.carnegiehall.org | subway: N, R 57 Street*

DAVID GEFFEN HALL ⭐
(151 D–E2) (*F5*)

The Avery Fisher Hall was built in 1962. In 2019 it is due for renovation, and because David Geffen, an entertainment tycoon worth $7 billion, has donated $100 million, the famous concert hall in the *Lincoln Center* already bears his name. Home of the world famous New York Philharmonic. *10 Lincoln Center/ 62nd Street | tel. 1 212 5 95 06 31 | lc. lincolncenter.org | subway: 1 66 Street*

PARK AVENUE ARMORY
(152 B3) (*H6*)

This arts centre in an iron structure dating from 1881 is impressively large and perfect for unusual performances, concerts and art exhibitions. It once even

A cathedral of culture – the world famous Met in the Lincoln Center

housed a fairground with a Ferris wheel! *643 Park Av./between 66th and 67th St. | www.armoryonpark.org | subway: 4, 5, 6 68 Street*

OPERA & BALLET

New York's largest opera house is the *Metropolitan Opera.* The Met is legendary and performing on its stage in the Lincoln Center is an honour even for the biggest stars. Rivalry is rampant in the ballet – the prominent *American Ballet Theatre* (ABT, *www.abt.org*) vies against the *New York City Ballet (www.nycballet. com)* which prefers to give up-and-coming artists their break.

CITY CENTER ⭐ (151 E4) (*ᗰF7*)
The theatre aims to attract as broad an audience as possible to the performing arts. So its range is wide, from dance and musicals to drama. *130 W 55th Street/ between 6th and 7th Av. | tel. 1 212 2 47 04 30 | www.nycitycenter.org | subway: N, R 57 Street*

DAVID H. KOCH THEATER
(151 E2) (*ᗰ F5*)
This 1960s building by the prominent architect Philip Johnson is home today to productions by the New York City Ballet. *20 Lincoln Center/62nd Street | tel. 1212 8 70 55 70 | www.davidhkochtheater.com | subway: 1 66 Street*

JOYCE THEATER (146 C3) (*ᗰ C10*)
The dance ensembles that perform their choreographies on the stage here come from all over the world. *175 8th Av./19th Street | tel. 1212 6919740 | www.joyce. org | subway: 1 18 Street*

METROPOLITAN OPERA ⭐
(151 E2) (*ᗰ E5*)
One of the most famous opera houses in the world, the Met was founded in 1883 by a group of millionaires. Not only operas but also the American Ballet Theatre performs on its stage. You can explore the house itself on a *backstage tour (during the season Mon– Sat 3pm, Sun 10:30am and 1:30pm |*

cost $25 | tel. 1 212 7 69 70 28). Lincoln Center/62nd–66th Street | tel. 1 212 3 62 60 00 | www.metopera.org | subway: 1 66 Street

TISCH SCHOOL OF THE ARTS
(143 E1) (∅ E13)
Why applaud only the well-known stars when there are also excellent up-and-coming dancers? Come and see tomorrow's stars in the making! Oct–May | $5 (donation) | 111 2nd Av. | 3rd floor | www.dance.tisch.nyu.edu | subway: F 2 Av.

THEATRES & OFF-BROADWAY

APOLLO THEATER (159 D2) (∅ 0)
This theatre in Harlem, built in 1914, hosts a talent show on Wednesdays for people with a thick skin: musicians and dancers, comedians and rappers expose themselves to the acclaim of the audience – or to booing and hissing! 253 W 125th Street | tel. 1 212 5 31 53 00 | www.apollo theater.com | subway: 125th Street, 2, 3

BLUE MAN GROUP (147 D5–6) (∅ D13)
Long running and world famous. The group started in 1991 and do performances pieces that take the mickey out of the arts scene. At the Astor Place Theatre (434 Lafayette Street/Astor Place | www.blueman.com | subway: 6 Astor Place

BROOKLYN ACADEMY OF MUSIC ★
(140 A4) (∅ I22)
Theatre and performance art venue. Composer Philip Glass, theatre director Robert Wilson and musician and performing artist Laurie Anderson are among those who staged pieces for this institution, which also has a cinema. 30 Lafayette Av./between St Felix Street and Ashland Place | Brooklyn | tel. 1 718 6 36 41 00 | www.bam.org | subway: 2–5, B, D, Q Atlantic Av.-Barclays Center

JOSEPH PAPP PUBLIC THEATER
(147 D5–6) (∅ D13)
You can see contemporary drama on several stages. If you prefer to tap your feet to music, in Joe's Pub (tel. 1 212 5 39 87 78 | www.joespub.com) soul ladies like Alicia Keys and Joss Stone perform. 425 Lafayette Street/Astor Place | tel. 1 212 9 67 75 55 | www.publictheater.org | subway: 6 Astor Place

THE KITCHEN
(146 B2) (∅ B10)
Centre for performance, dance and video art, as well as literary events, discussions with artists and readings – serious, innovative, exciting. 512 W 19th Street/between 10th and 11th Av. | tel. 1 212 2 55 57 93 | www.thekitchen.org | subway: C, E 23 Street

FOR TV SERIES FANS

Mad Men – An award-winning television series that is set in the New York of the 1960s – full of dramas of success and social upheaval unfold in a world of advertising and glamour

Girls – Four girlfriends caught between their careers, men and the insanity of life in New York – sounds like "Sex and the City", but the girls in Lena Dunham's TV series (2012–2017) are still in their mid-20s, and their lives are tough

WHERE TO STAY

New York is expensive. Hotel rooms for under $100 a night are almost extinct; the average is between $300 and $400. 50 million visitors a year are the reason for this. The rule of thumb is to book early – preferably online where you tend to get the best offers. Room prices fluctuate seasonally and an overnight stay is cheaper in January, February, July and August.

It is customary in the United States to quote accommodation prices per room and not per person. If two people share a room, i.e. a double, it is generally not more expensive than a single. When you plan your budget remember that on top of the quote you will be levied an additional surcharge of 14.75 per cent in Hotel Sales Tax and additional $3.50 per night room tax. All-inclusive packages with accommodation and flights booked in Europe are often cheaper.

The chambermaid is entitled to a tip of at least $5 for long stays, $1 per day in more basic hotels, $2 per day in more expensive hotels. The concierge service in good hotels will assist you with reservations at sought-after restaurants and get you opera and theatre tickets.

For hotel information and internet bookings go to: *www.hotelsnewyork.com* | *www.newyorkhotelspecials.com* | *www.nyc.com/hotels/*. It is becoming increasingly popular to book an apartment or room rented privately by New Yorkers. A wide array of websites offer all kinds of accommodations sorted according to price range and neighbourhood. Popu-

In the city that never sleeps, your choice of hotel is important: within walking distance to a theatre or right in the heart of the nightlife?

lar sites include *www.airbnb.com, www.roomorama.com* and *www.nyhabitat.com* (for details, see p. 104).

HOTELS: EXPENSIVE

BOWERY HOTEL
(143 E1) (*D14*)
Velvet-covered armchairs, Moroccan tiles, marble fireplaces and oriental carpets adorn this attractive 135-roomed designer hotel in the sought-after Lower East Side. *335 Bowery | tel. 1212 5 05 91 00 | www.theboweryhotel.com | subway: F 2 Av.; 6 Bleecker Street*

CROSBY STREET HOTEL
(143 D1) (*D14*)
The elegant, hip SoHo hotel is located on a cobbled street and has a lovely roof garden. The rooms have individual designs, some black-and-white, others flowery – skilfully and playfully done. *86 rooms | 79 Crosby Street | tel. 1212 2 26 64 00 |*

A night on the town awaits – but so does a tasteful room in Hotel Gansevoort

www.firmdalehotels.com | subway: R Prince Street, 6 Spring Street

HOTEL GANSEVOORT ☼

(146 B3) (*Ⓜ B11*)

186 spacious rooms in the Meatpacking District – right at the heart of New York's nightlife. Illuminated bathroom doors, huge TV screens and lavish fittings. Dine outdoors, visit the *Plunge Bar* or the pool on the roof. *18 9th Av./13th Street | tel. 1212 2 06 67 00 | www.hotelgansevoort. com | subway: A, C, E, L 14 Street/8 Av.*

THE GREENWICH HOTEL

(142 B2) (*Ⓜ B15*)

Modern, elegant and tastefully furnished. Robert De Niro's upscale hotel in TriBeCa displays his keen sense of design. *75 rooms, 13 suites | 377 Greenwich Street | tel. 1212 9 41 86 00 | www.thegreenwich hotel.com | subway: 1 Franklin Street*

INSIDER TIP ▶ THE HIGHLINE HOTEL

(146 B2) (*Ⓜ C10*)

A recently established and likeable hotel in a historic college building with lots of charm. The rooms are generously sized

by New York standards. The courtyard is a haven of peace in Chelsea, and a coffee truck serves drinks in the pretty front garden. You can explore the area with the hotel bikes. Plenty of galleries and restaurants are close by, and the nightlife is just around the corner. *60 rooms | 180 10th Av./near 20th St. | tel. 1212 9 29 38 88 | www.thehighlinehotel.com | subway: C, E 23 Street*

THE HOTEL ON RIVINGTON ★

(143 E2) (*Ⓜ E15*)

A hotel that is fitting for the Lower East Side boom. A hi-tech glass tower with 21 floors of minimalist décor and a real panorama effect in the rooms. *110 rooms | 107 Rivington Street/between Essex Street and Ludlow Street | tel. 1212 4 75 26 00 | www.hotelonrivington.com | subway: F Delancey Street*

HUDSON HOTEL ★ ☼

(151 D–E3) (*Ⓜ F6*)

Two bars and a restaurant are noisy meeting places for chic guests. More tranquil: a breakfast in the courtyard. Deluxe chill-out place: the Sky Terrace on the 15th floor! *1,000 rooms | 358 W 58th Street/between 8th and 9th Av. | tel. 1212 5 54 60 00 | www.hudsonhotel. com | subway: A–D, 159 Street-Columbus Circle*

THE MARRIOTT MARQUIS ☆
(151 D5) *(ⓜ E8)*

A futuristic building featuring plenty of glass in the midst of the illuminations on Times Square – for a true New York feeling. *The View* restaurant on the 47th floor is revolving and offers fantastic views also to non-guests. With its *prix fixe menu* of *$84*, this culinary experience is not cheap but good value for money. *1,886 rooms | 1535 Broadway/between 45th and 46th Street | tel. 1212 3 98 19 00 | www.nymarriottmarquis.com | subway: N, R, 1–3 42 Street/Times Square*

THE PENINSULA (152 A4) *(ⓜ G10)*

Stylishly fitted out with Asian antiques. On the top floors there is a luxurious health club and a pool with a view, on the roof the *Salon de Ning* bar (see p. 87). *240 rooms | doubles from approx. $695 | 700 5th Av./55th Street | tel. 1212 9 56 28 88 | www.peninsula.com | subway: E, M, N, R 5 Av.*

THE ST REGIS
(152 A4) *(ⓜ G7)*

This art-nouveau townhouse was built in 1904. Over 100 years later it is synonymous with elegance, a landmark on the New York hotel scene. *256 rooms | doubles from approx. $695 | 2 E 55th Street/5th Av. | tel. 1212 7 53 45 00 | www.stregisnewyork.com | subway: E, M 5 Avenue*

THE STANDARD ☆

Looming large and unmistakable, the ⭐ *Standard High Line* stretches across the High Line as if on stilts. *Le Bain* on the rooftop is ideal for a cocktail stop. Hotelier André Balazs' prestigious hotel with its

⭐ **The Hotel on Rivington**
Floor to ceiling windows and unrivalled views of Manhattan's in-district, the Lower East Side
→ p. 98

⭐ **Hudson Hotel**
Great views across the Hudson and very cool design and décor
→ p. 98

⭐ **The Standard High Line**
A hip hotel that straddles the High Line Park in a bold arc
→ p. 99

⭐ **Room Mate Grace Hotel**
Times Square is just around the corner, the pool and its bar are open all night, and the rooms are full of unusual ideas in New York style
→ p. 101

⭐ **The Redbury NY**
For everyone who likes music and contrasts of red and black: following a facelift, the hotel celebrates New York as the birthplace of rock 'n' roll and pop – sensational!
→ p. 102

⭐ **The Harlem Flophouse**
Guests have their finger on the pulse of Harlem yet are quickly in Manhattan. This restored townhouse with lots of atmosphere, a hotel since 1917, is a trip back in time → p. 103

MARCO POLO HIGHLIGHTS

hip interiors in the trendy Meatpacking District offers spectacular views across the Hudson. The branch on Cooper Square is modern and stylish. Tom Cruise's ex-wife Katie Holmes held a party on the roof of this glass and steel tower. The view is amazing and the East Village lies at your feet. *The Standard High Line (146 B3) (B11): 337 rooms | 848 Washington Street | tel. 1212 6 45 46 46 | subway: A, C, E 14 Street; The Standard East Village (147 E6) (E13): 144 rooms | 25 Cooper Square | tel. 1212 4 75 57 00 | subway: 6 Astor Place. www.standardhotels.com*

HOTELS: MODERATE

ACE HOTEL

(147 E2) (*E10*)

This hip and reasonably priced hotel was designed by Roman & Williams, interior designers to Gwyneth Paltrow and Kate Hudson. The firm's signature is combining unusual objects salvaged from old houses with vintage furniture. The definition of trendy it also has a bar with some hip DJs. *260 rooms | 20 W 29th Street | tel. 1212 6 79 22 22 | www.acehotel.com | subway: B, D, F, N, Q, R 34 Street-Herald Square*

MORE THAN A GOOD NIGHT'S SLEEP

Stay in a cabin!

In 1912 the survivors of the Titanic spent some time in INSIDER TIP *The Jane Hotel* **(146 B4)** (***B11***) *(211 rooms | 113 Jane Street/between Washington and W Street | tel. 1212 9 24 67 00 | www.thejanenyc.com | subway: A, C, E, L 14 Street)*. The tiny rooms of this historic house with a view of the Hudson River look like ship's cabins. Fresh bedding only once a week. Single room $99, double room $250, ask about weekly rates.

Wind and waves

Go surfing in the morning, then take an hour's ride on the subway to Manhattan: INSIDER TIP *Truckafloat* **(159 F5)** (***0***) *(from $80 | 59–14 Beach Channel Drive | Marina 59 | www.truckafloat.com | subway: A Beach 60 Street)*, probably New York's most unconventional hotel, consists of small houseboats in the Rockaways, for a wave-bobbing, low-cost overnight stay.

Eye to eye with Lady Liberty

The *Ritz-Carlton Battery Park* **(142 A5)** (***A17***) *(298 rooms | double room from $345 | 2 W Street | tel. 1212 3 44 08 00 | www.ritzcarlton.com | subway: 1 South Ferry, 4, 5 Bowling Green)* is New York's first luxury hotel with stunning views of New York harbour. At night, the chambermaid points the telescope towards the Statue of Liberty.

Don't work, sleep

In Queens the INSIDER TIP *Paper Factory* **(159 D3)** (***0***) *(123 rooms | 36 Street 3706 | Queens | tel. 1718 3 92 72 00 | www.paperfactoryhotel.com | subway: M, R 36 Street)* is a particularly cool hotel: you sleep in a former factory between vintage mopeds, a huge tower of books, heavy wooden furniture and leather sofas. There is lots of space and a roof terrace. The subway is just around the corner, only two stops from Manhattan.

WHERE TO STAY

INSIDERTIP COLONIAL HOUSE INN
(146 C2) (*C10*)

This brownstone building with 22 rooms (some of them with en-suite bathroom) dates back to 1850 and there is a rooftop area that is a great place to relax. It is particularly popular with the gay community. The cheapest rooms cost $180 while those with an en-suite bathroom go for a little more. *318 W 22nd Street/8th Av. | tel. 1212 243 96 69 | www.colonial houseinn.com | subway: C, E 23 Street*

HOTEL EAST HOUSTON
(143 E1) (*E14*)

This modern affordable hotel is ideally located to explore the Lower East Side scene. The rooms are not big but stylishly decorated. The hotel is in an area full of restaurants, bars, cafés, small shops and galleries. It also has a roof terrace. *42 rooms | 151 E Houston Street | tel. 1212 777 00 12 | www.hoteleasthouston.com | subway: F 2 Av., B, D, F Broadway-Lafayette*

ROOM MATE GRACE HOTEL ★
(151 D5) (*F8*)

A hotel with style: Simple but first-rate rooms, breakfast included, a sauna to relax after a busy day out and a pool with bar where you can swim any time of night. So pack your swimming costume! Perfectly situated close to the hustle and bustle of Times Square, MoMA and the Rockefeller Center. *140 rooms | 125 W 45th Street/between 6th and 7th Av. | tel. 1212 3 54 23 23 | www.room-matehotels. com | subway: B, D, F, M Rockefeller Center*

KIMPTON INK48 ✂
(150 B4) (*D6*)

This new boutique hotel in Hell's Kitchen offers spectacular views across the Hudson and a number of services including music systems with iPod docking stations, stylish rooms, a spa and a gym.

222 rooms | 652 11th Av. | tel. 1212 7 57 00 88 | www.ink48.com | subway: C, E, 1 50 Street

MARRAKECH HOTEL
(155 D2) (*0*)

This Upper West Side hotel does justice to its name with a casual Moroccan and

Modern design is a permanent guest at The Standard

oriental feel to it. The rooms are small but have internet access. *127 rooms | 2688 Broadway/103rd Street | tel. 1212 2 22 29 54 | www.marrakechhotelnyc.com | subway: 1 103 Street*

OUT (150 C5) (*D7*)

Only two blocks from Times Square, this low-cost hotel provides rooms for a sleep-share with up to three others (bunks and TV). From $59, often more expensive. Double rooms costs more. Sauna and jacuzzi. Note: **INSIDER TIP** Don't book the room above the bar. *105 rooms | 510 W 42nd Street | tel. 1212 9 47 29 99 | theoutnyc.com | subway: A, C, E 42 Street-Port Authority*

INSIDER TIP ▸ THE POD HOTEL

A bunk here is yours for the night from $180. Small, affordable rooms – some with bunk beds – minimally furnished plus free internet access and a rooftop garden. The clientèle is young and seemingly hip. The first Pod Hotel was so successful that the owners have built a second one in Manhattan. Rooms at Pod 39 start at $205. *Pod 51 (152 B6) (Ⓜ H8): 156 rooms | 230 E 51st Street/between 2nd and 3rd Av. | tel. 1212 3 55 03 00 | subway: 6 51 Street);* The Pod 39 Hotel *(148 A1) (Ⓜ G9): 366 rooms | 145 E 39th Street/between 3rd and Lexington Av. |* tel. 1212 8 65 57 00 | subway: S, 4–7 Grand Central-42 Street | www.thepodhotel.com

THE REDBURY NY ★ (147 F2) (Ⓜ F10) This hotel (it used to be called the Martha Washington) has style and New York atmosphere, yet is usually not expensive. The change of name came along with a makeover inside, now intended to be reminiscent of the years of Tin Pan Alley, the streets around here where the American music business got started from about 1890. Red and black are the dominant colours in rooms that have an interesting layout, skilfully disguising their small size. The Empire State Building is just around the corner. Crispy pizza is served in Marta. *261 rooms | 29 E 29th Street/between Park and Madison Av. |* tel. 1212 6 89 19 00 | www.theredbury. com | subway: 6 28 Street

The Washington Square Hotel in Greenwich Village has lots of atmosphere

INSIDER TIP **SANKOFA ABAN**
(159 D4) (*m* 0)

A brownstone dating from 1880 in Bedford-Stuyvesant, a fashionable part of Brooklyn, houses this delightful bed & breakfast. The owners have six rooms for guests and put on jazz concerts. *6 rooms | 107 Macon Street | tel. 1917 7 04 92 37 | sankofaaban.com | subway: A, C Nostrand Avenue*

WASHINGTON SQUARE HOTEL
(146 C5) (*m* C12)

A good value for money hotel located in Greenwich Village where you can also enjoy jazz brunch on a Sunday. *160 rooms | 103 Waverly Place/MacDougal Street | tel. 1212 7 77 95 15 | www.washingtonsquare hotel.com | subway: A–F, M W 4 Street*

WYTHE HOTEL (145 D2) (*m* J14)

The Wythe Hotel with its cool industrial design is situated in an old brick factory on the banks of the East River in trendy Williamsburg. It offers a mix of stylish lofts with a view of Manhattan and rooms for small groups. *70 rooms | 80 N 11th Street/N 11th Street | Brooklyn | tel. 1718 4 60 80 01 | www.wythehotel. com | subway: L Bedford Av.*

HOTELS: BUDGET

CARLTON ARMS
(147 F3) (*m* F11)

A little antiquated but its rooms are charming and are all designed by a different artist – in fact there is art all over the hotel. If you stay more than a night you will have to make your own bed but for $160 (or as little as $130 if you are willing to share a bathroom) it is a bargain. No TV. *52 rooms | 160 E 25th Street/between 3rd Av. and Lexington Av. | tel. 1212 6 79 06 80 | www.carltonarms.com | subway: 6 23 Street*

EAST VILLAGE BED & COFFEE
(144 A1) (*m* F14)

Very friendly guesthouse with a small garden. Every room has a different theme (French Room, Zen Room etc). No-frills ambience. Free bike rentals. Double room from $140. *10 rooms | 110 Av. C | tel. 1212 5 33 41 75 | www.bedandcoffee.com | subway: 6 Astor Place*

THE HARLEM FLOPHOUSE ★
(158 C2) (*m* 0)

This beautifully refurbished townhouse almost comes across as an art gallery thanks to the passion of its owner Rene Calvo who collects art from Harlem. On offer at this B&B are four quiet, comfortable rooms with two bathrooms and the price is $150 on your own, $175 for two people. Ceiling fans instead of air-conditioning add to the sense of calm in the rooms. WiFi is included in the price and in summer you may even be invited to an impromptu barbecue. Its location in northern Manhattan makes for an ideal opportunity to explore Harlem in all its diversity. *242 W 123rd Street/between Frederick Douglass Blvd. and 7th Av. | tel. 1347 6 32 19 60 | www.harlemflophouse. com | subway: A–D 125 Street*

HERALD SQUARE HOTEL
(147 E2) (*m* E 10)

This used to be *Life* magazine's editorial office. Today it is a very popular and affordable hotel. *120 rooms | 19 W 31st Street/between 5th Av. and Broadway | tel. 1 866 8 33 09 88 | www.heraldsquare hotel.com | subway: B, D, F, N, Q, R 34 Street-Herald Square*

LARCHMONT HOTEL
(147 D4–5) (*m* D12)

Thanks to its good value and quiet location north of Washington Square, charmingly old-fashioned Larchmont is very much in demand – there are many European guests. A small kitchen and shared bathrooms on every floor. Double rooms from $140. Breakfast is included in the price. *62 rooms | 27 W 11th Street/5th Av. | tel. 1 212 989 93 33 | www.larchmont hotel.com | subway: A, B, C, D, E, F, M W 4 Street*

HOTEL LE BLEU
(139 F6) (*ØJ J24*)

Like the colour of its name, this hotel in Brooklyn has a rather cool look. But it offers a lot for relatively little (by New York standards): internet access, breakfast, a minibar and even a small balcony. It may be lo-

cated in an industrial area but only a block away is Brooklyn's Fifth Avenue with its many restaurants, bars and shops; Prospect Park is only one subway station away. *48 rooms | 370 4th Av./4th Street | tel. 1 718 625 15 00 | www.hotellebleu.com | subway: F, G, R 4 Av.-9th Street*

HOTEL NEWTON
(154 C3) (*ØJ G1*)

Close to Central Park this unassuming hotel has exceptionally large clean rooms at affordable prices and friendly service. Suites come equipped with a microwave oven, mini fridge and iron. Children up to the age of 17 can stay INSIDERTIP► in the same room as their parents free of charge. *110 rooms | 2528 E Broadway/95th Street | tel. 1 212 6 78 65 00 | www.thehotelnewon.com | subway: 1–3 96 Street*

MORNINGSIDE INN
(155 D1) (*ØJ 0*)

Plain clean rooms in a renovated house exuding an old-world New York charm. Weekly and monthly rates also available. *85 rooms | | 235 W 107th Street/between Broadway and Amsterdam Av. | tel. 1 212 3 16 00 55 | www.morningsideinn-ny.com | subway: 1 110 Street*

OFF SOHO SUITES
(143 E2) (*ØJ E15*)

The ideal district to experience Downtown on a budget and your own kitchenette will help cut down on costs. *38 rooms | 11 Rivington Street/between The Bowery and Chrystie Street | tel. 1 212 9 79 98 15 | www.offsoho.com | subway: F 2 Av.*

RIFF CHELSEA
(147 D1) (*ØJ D9*)

A great address for people with a tight budget. The *superior rooms* are a bit more expensive, but come with a DVD

LOW BUDGET

Apartments can be a good alternative to a hotel, often less expensive and more comfortable. Contact *New York Habitat (tel. 1 212 2 55 80 18 | www.nyhabitat.com), City Lights (tel. 1 212 7 37 70 49 | www.citylightsbandb.com), Affordable New York (tel. 1 212 5 33 40 01 | www.affordablenewyork city.com), www.9flats.com* or *www.roomorama.com.*

You can often get accommodation cheaper from individual hotel websites or booking agencies such as *www.hoteldiscount.com* or *www.quikbook.com.*

Private apartments can be found, for example, at *www.airbnb.com.* There are also private listings on *newyork.craigslist.org.* With all these types of ads, however, you should be careful because there are some internet fraud schemes on the net!

At Hotel Le Bleu even the bedding fits the name

player. Double rooms with shared bath from $139 and doubles with private bath from $189. *44 rooms | 300 W 30th Street/8th Av. | tel. 1 212 2 44 78 27 | www.riffhotels.com | subway: A, C, E 34 Street*

HOSTELS & CO.

HOSTELLING INTERNATIONAL
(155 D2) (*Ø O*)

Affordable, basic and clean. From $49 you can have a bed in a six-bed dorm, WiFi and breakfast included. *672 beds, 5 single rooms, 15 4-bed dorms | 891 Amsterdam Av./between 103rd and 104th Street | tel. 1 212 9 32 23 00 | www.hinewyork.org | subway: 1 103 Street*

KOLPING HOUSE
(156 B6) (*Ø K3*)

Only for men between the ages of 21 and 35; suitable for longer stays. A week costs just $255 (single room with one warm meal per day from Mon to Fri). Two simple letters of reference from a school, university or employer are required. *88 rooms | 165 E 88th Street/Lexington Av. | tel. 1 212 3 69 66 47 | www.kolpingny.org | subway: 4, 5, 6 86 Street*

VANDERBILT YMCA
(152 B6) (*Ø G 8*)

You will find a YMCA in just about every borough of New York. There are three in Manhattan, two in Brooklyn and two in Queens. Depending on availability you can opt to sleep in a mini single room or in rooms for two, three or four persons. Communal bathroom. Single rooms from $123, double from $160. The nicest and also the most centrally located is the Vanderbilt, which even has a pool. *370 beds | 224 E 47th Street/between 2nd and 3rd Av. | tel. 1 212 9 12 25 00 | www.ymcanyc.org | subway: 4–7 Grand Central*

DISCOVERY TOURS

① NEW YORK AT A GLANCE

START: ① Eisenberg's
END: ⑮ Rockwood Music Hall

Distance:
🚶 30 km/18.6 miles

1 day
Driving/walking time
(without stops)
3.5 hours

COSTS: entrance fees $57, speedboat *The Beast* $29, food and drinks $50, taxi approx. $12

IMPORTANT TIPS: avoid the long lines at the Empire State Building by purchasing tickets online (more expensive). Buy a weekly ticket for the subway ($31). Eisenberg's doesn't open until 9am on Sat/Sun. *The Beast* only late Apr to end Sept

New York at its best – from an authentic diner breakfast to the different boroughs and the tallest skyscrapers to the most authentic club.

Would you like to explore the places that are unique to this city? Then the Discovery Tours are just the thing for you – they include terrific tips for stops worth making, breathtaking places to visit, selected restaurants and fun activities. It's even easier with the Touring App: download the tour with map and route to your smartphone using the QR Code on pages 2/3 or from the website address in the footer below – and you'll never get lost again even when you're offline. → p. 2/3

TOURING APP

→ p. 2/3

08:00am Thanks to the time change, you will probably be starving when you wake up on your first morning in New York. At ❶ **Eisenberg's** → p. 62 – a traditional diner **in Chelsea (subway N, R 23 Street)** – eggs and different kinds of toast are made to order. If you sit at the counter, you can watch how fast the cooks and waitstaff work. Once you've cleaned your plate, **walk north on Fifth Avenue, past one of New York's real landmarks, the Flatiron Building (on the right near 23rd Street),** which looks like an upright clothes iron. Shortly thereafter, you will come

❶ Eisenberg's 🍴

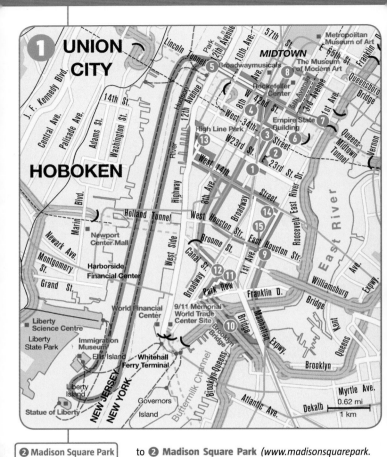

UNION CITY

MIDTOWN

HOBOKEN

■ Metropolitan
Museum of Art

The Museum
of Modern Art

Rockefeller
Center

Broadwaymusicals ⑤

⑧

W 42nd St.

West 34th ⑧

West-34th. ④

Empire State
Building

③ ⑥ ⑦

High Line Park

W23rd St. ⓵

E 23rd St. Dr.

⑬

West 14th ⓵

West Houston Str.

Broome St. ⑭

⑮

Canal St. East Houston Str.

⑨

Broadway ⑫

Park Row ⑪

9/11 Memorial
World Trade
Center Site

Franklin D.

⑩

Holland Tunnel

Newport
Center Mall

Harborside
Financial Center

World Financial
Center

Liberty
Science Centre

Liberty
State Park

Immigration
Museum

Ellis Island

Whitehall
Ferry Terminal

Liberty
Island

Statue of Liberty

NEW JERSEY
NEW YORK

Governors
Island

Brooklyn

Myrtle Ave.

Atlantic Ave.

Dekalb

0.62 mi

1 km

② Madison Square Park

to ② **Madison Square Park** *(www.madisonsquarepark. org)* with its modern sculptures **on the right-hand side between 23rd and 26th Street.**

③ Empire State Building

`09:00am` After another ten blocks, you will reach your destination, namely the ③ **Empire State Building** → p. 41 on 34th Street. With the high-speed elevator, you can whiz up to the platform on the 86th floor to take in the amazing view of the city from up high.

④ Times Square

`10:30am` Then head to 42nd Street to get to ④ **Times Square** → p. 26. Be dazzled by the colourful lights of the billboards competing for your attention – take a little break on the steps of the pedestrian-friendly square. But, don't sit down for too long because it's time to hop aboard "The Beast", the speedboat of **⑤ Circle Line Sightseeing Cruises** → p. 128. The tour **departs from the dock on the Hudson River *(pier 83, West 42nd Street)*, about a 20-minutes' walk away.** For half an hour, the boat speeds towards downtown, swinging past the Statue of Liberty → p. 33 before turning back.

12:30pm Walk back to Times Square and take the S-Train to the amazingly beautiful **⑥ Grand Central Terminal** → p. 42. **Climb up to the gallery** and look down on the bustling crowds of people hurrying to catch their trains. Hungry? At the **⑦ Grand Central Dining Concourse on the lower level,** there are almost three dozen dining options serving all kinds of food from around the world. **Back outside, stroll down Park Avenue – surrounded by expensive residential buildings – until you come to 53rd Street. Turn left to head to the ⑧ Museum of Modern Art** → p. 43. Even if you are not a fan of modern art, you should still explore the INSIDER TIP lovely Sculpture Garden and stop for a little break next to Picasso's "She-Goat" sculpture outside.

03:30pm By now you are probably hungry (again). **So, take the subway to the Lower East Side *(M-Train on 53rd Street to 2nd Avenue).* Just a few steps away, on Houston Street, is the famous ⑨ Katz Deli** *(205 E Houston Street/ Ludlow Street | www.katzdelicatessen.com)* with its huge trademark pastrami sandwiches.

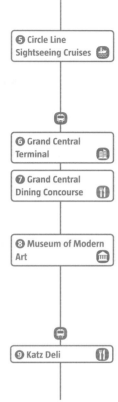

⑤ Circle Line Sightseeing Cruises

⑥ Grand Central Terminal

⑦ Grand Central Dining Concourse

⑧ Museum of Modern Art

⑨ Katz Deli

Old and new landmarks: the Statue of Liberty and One World Trade Center

- 🚌
- ⑩ Brooklyn Bridge 🚶
- ⑪ Chinatown 💬 🛍️
- ⑫ Canal Street 🛍️
- 🚲
- 🚌
- ⑬ High Line Park 🚲 ❄️ 🌳
- 🚌
- ⑭ Momofuku Ssäm Bar 🍴
- ⑮ Rockwood Music Hall 🎵 🍸

04:00pm Hop back on the subway and ride to Brooklyn *(stop: York Street),* so that you can walk across the ⑩ **Brooklyn Bridge** → p. 30. It is much more interesting to walk towards the Manhattan skyline rather than away from it! The new Frank Gehry Building, the Beekman Tower, glistens at the end of the bridge while the Statue of Liberty seems to wink as ships and ferries of all sizes chug under the bridge.

05:00pm Once you're on the other side of the river, stroll through ⑪ **Chinatown** → p. 34. This is an exotic experience with smells, sounds and a bustle to make you feel as if you were in Beijing. Little restaurants, food stores and shops selling knick-knacks announce their presence in Chinese characters. Shop for handbags, glasses and jewellery on ⑫ **Canal Street** → p. 36 and test your bartering skills! Keep a look out for a Chinese *massage shop* → p. 32 and do something good for your back and tired feet.

06:00pm From Canal Street, take the subway to 14th Street. The charming ⑬ **High Line Park** → p. 22 was built on the site of a former overhead railway. Some of the old tracks still exist, but now indigenous grasses grow between them and the wooden deckchairs are a great place to relax for a bit. The view over lovely Greenwich Village with its brownstone houses is fascinating – including the Hudson River and New Jersey in the background.

An unforgettable walk over the Brooklyn Bridge towards Manhattan

07:30pm Hail a cab and zoom over to the East Village to the ⑭ **Momofuku Ssäm Bar** → p. 66, where the out-of-the-ordinary meat dishes are so tasty that your eyes will light up.

09:00pm Do you still have a bit of energy left? **Then walk a couple of blocks south to the ⑮ Rockwood Music Hall** → p. 90. Undiscovered musicians still play in little clubs like this one. Order a drink and enjoy the truly intimate atmosphere and some good music.

2 STRANGE WORLDS

START: ❶ Washington Square
END: ⓯ Veselka

6 hours
Walking time
(without stops)
1 hour

Distance:
➡ 4 km/2.5 miles

COSTS: entrance fees and food $50

This walking tour of SoHo, Little Italy, Chinatown and the East Village will take you to the prettiest places in downtown New York. Get a taste for the architecture, contemporary art and colourful mix of people – from Chinese immigrants to Mexican musicians to Ghanian students – that make New York such a cosmopolitan place.

10:00am The starting point of the tour is ❶ **Washington Square** → p. 40 with its victory arch where students from the neighbouring New York University (NYU) often hang out. Street jugglers and musicians perform as dogs romp around the fenced-in dog playground and chess players face off in the southwestern corner of the park. **Cross over Bleecker Street,** once the centre of the folk music scene in the 1960s, **and follow West Houston Street to one of the city's most interesting architectural districts:** ❷ **SoHo** → p. 34. Some of the cast-iron buildings – for-mer multi-floor factories, shops and warehouses – still line the old cobblestone streets. They were rediscovered by artists and students in the 1960s who converted them into huge lofts like those in the former home of the sculptor Donald Judd. **In this building at** ❸ **101 Spring Street** *(tours Tue, Thu, Fri at 1pm, 3pm, 5pm; book on the website in advance | costs $25.50 | www.juddfoundation.org)* works by Judd, Dan Flavin, Claes Oldenburg and others are on display. **Wander along Spring Street, browse in the boutiques or do a little people watching a block to the north of Spring Street in Little Italy** at the trendy ❹ **Cafe Gitane** *(242 Mott Street | www.cafegitanenyc.com)*.

12:00pm Spring Street runs into ❺ **Broadway** → p. 35 at its eastern end where there are plenty of shops. **Walk to-wards uptown** and take a look around in **Prada** → p. 78. **At the gourmet temple** ❻ **Dean & DeLuca** → p. 75,

❶ Washington Square

❷ SoHo

❸ 101 Spring Street

❹ Cafe Gitane

❺ Broadway

❻ Dean & DeLuca

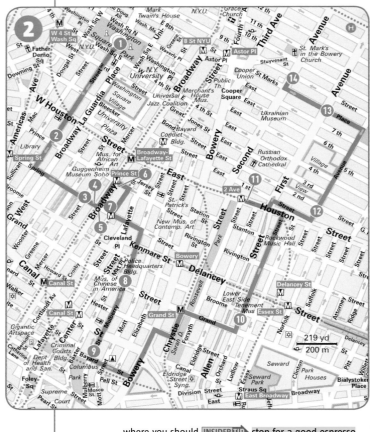

where you should INSIDER TIP stop for a good espresso,
**turn around and walk back to the south. Return to Spring
Street,** and follow in the footsteps of prominent New Yorkers: For those looking to spot a film star or a model, the
bistro ❼ Balthazar → p. 84 is a good bet.

**Walk two blocks to the east on Spring Street and then
go right on Mulberry Street,** the main street of ❽ Little
Italy → p. 34. The cluster of Italian restaurants towered
over by 100-year-old tenement buildings with exterior
fire escapes is struggling to survive because ❾ Chinatown → p. 34 is expanding to the north, threatening to
encroach upon Little Italy. Canal Street, however, is still

❼ Balthazar

❽ Little Italy

❾ Chinatown

the Chinese distribution hub for fish, meat and vegetables where mobile vendors peddle samples.

Turn left down Bowery Street, then follow Grand Street and Orchard Street to another district in flux: the ⑩ **Lower East Side** → p. 37 has gotten a face-lift. Jewish immigrants from Eastern Europe once dominated this part of the city in the 19th century. Synagogues, groceries and restaurants still attest to their influence, but hip bars, lots of restaurants and boutiques have pushed out many of the Jewish influences. **Make sure to visit the ⑪ Yonah Schimmel Knish Bakery** *(www.knishery.com)* **on Houston Street** and try a spinach knish, a savoury filled dumpling of East European origin – a bite of the old Lower East Side.

`02:00pm` **To the north of Houston Street,** the contrasts never end. Beginning in the 1850s, many German immigrants moved into the simple apartments in the heart of the ⑫ **East Village** → p. 37, earning the area the nickname "Little Germany". **Avenue A and Tompkins Square Park** were a stronghold of the hippies in the 1960s and the punk rock scene in the 1970s. Today this neighbourhood is home to young creative professionals, bankers and lawyers. **One of the last stops for the day is ⑬ St Marks Place** → p. 40 with its `INSIDER TIP` alluring little boutiques. **When you come to 2nd Avenue, take a little**

⑩ Lower East Side

⑪ Yonah Schimmel Knish Bakery

⑫ East Village

⑬ St Marks Place

Some places in Little Italy still look like part of a film set

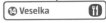 ⑭ Veselka 🍴

detour to the north. In ⑭ **Veselka → p. 40 on the corner of 9th Street**, the food is Russian-Ukrainian, which you can taste in the form of delicious pancakes with a cream cheese filling called *blintzes*.

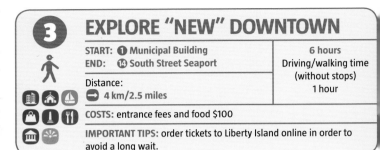

3 — EXPLORE "NEW" DOWNTOWN

START: ① Municipal Building END: ⑭ South Street Seaport	6 hours Driving/walking time (without stops) 1 hour
Distance: ➜ 4 km/2.5 miles	

COSTS: entrance fees and food $100

IMPORTANT TIPS: order tickets to Liberty Island online in order to avoid a long wait.

The face of the southern tip of Manhattan has changed greatly over the last few years, especially with the completion of the 9/11 Memorial commemorating the terrorist attacks on 11 September 2001 and the highest skyscraper in the western world at One World Trade Center. This tour will also take you to a number of other sites, including one of New York's most famous landmarks, the Statue of Liberty.

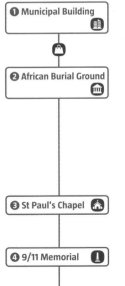

① Municipal Building 📄

② African Burial Ground 🏛

③ St Paul's Chapel 🏠

④ 9/11 Memorial ❗

09:30am From the ① **Municipal Building → p. 31, located on subway line R, walk to Duane Park**. The antique shops you find here today will give you an impression of how the merchants who built up the southern tip of Manhattan in the late 18th century once lived. **The corner of Duane Street and Broadway is home to the ② INSIDER TIP African Burial Ground** *(290 Broadway | www.nps.gov/afbg)*, an old cemetery in which an estimated 15,000 slaves from Africa are buried. You can learn more about the history of this site, first rediscovered in 1991, at the Visitors' Center. **From here, walk further south to New York's City Hall → p. 31**, which was built between 1803 and 1812. The near-by Woolworth Building *(233 Broadway/between Barclay Street and Park Place)* with its green copper tip is a real eye-catcher. **Manhattan's only colonial era church, ③ St Paul's Chapel → p. 32, is located on Vesey Street. This small chapel was a saving grace for the exhausted helpers who were at the scene following the World Trade Center attacks. Walk along Vesey Street to get to the former Ground Zero,** now the site of the impressive ④ **9/11 Memorial → p. 29** with its two black-rimmed pools bearing the engraved names of all the victims. Take a moment to re-

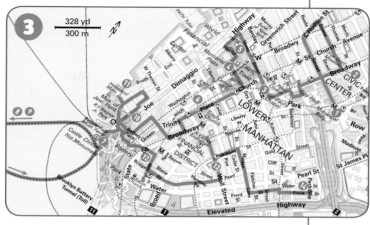

flect and listen to the waterfalls in this special space. There is also a good view of **One World Trade Center** → p. 32 from here. The ❺ **One World Observatory** (oneworldobservatory.com) is the highest lookout point in the city.

01:00pm Once you are back on the ground, **walk south on Church Street, past ❻ Trinity Church**, which crouches between the tall buildings of the financial district. **Shortly before you come to the south end of Broadway**, the famous charging bronze bull on Wall Street symbolizing a strong, optimistic financial market scrapes at the ground with its hooves. The view of the tree-lined avenue running to the south from **Battery Place and First Place** is fantastic. You can capture one of New York's most famous landmarks – the Statue of Liberty – together with Ellis Island and Verrazano Bridge with just one click of your camera.

You can get even closer to Lady Liberty by heading to ❼ Castle Clinton, where immigrants to the New World were received until 1860, **to board the ferry to the ❽ Statue of Liberty** → p. 33. First enjoy the view of the statue from afar and then climb up to the viewing platform in the crown. **Continue on to ❾ Ellis Island** → p. 31, the island which immigrants had to pass through after 1860.

03:00pm After you return to the mainland, you can decide whether you want to visit one of the three museums that you will pass on your way through Battery

❺ One World Observatory

❻ Trinity Church

❼ Castle Clinton

❽ Statue of Liberty

❾ Ellis Island

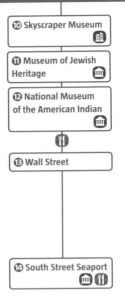

⑩ Skyscraper Museum

⑪ Museum of Jewish Heritage

⑫ National Museum of the American Indian

⑬ Wall Street

⑭ South Street Seaport

Park to Wall Street: the ⑩ **Skyscraper Museum** → p. 32, the ⑪ **Museum of Jewish Heritage** → p. 31 or the ⑫ **National Museum of the American Indian** → p. 32. Then delve into the world of brokers and investors. **At the corner of Broad Street and Pearl Street, look for Fraunces Tavern** *(54 Pearl Street | tel. 1 212 9 68 17 76 | www.frauncestavern.com | Moderate–Expensive)*, a restaurant established in 1763 in which you can order a typical New York *strip steak*. From **Pearl Street, turn left down** ⑬ **Wall Street** → p. 34, home of the **Stock Exchange** → p. 33 *(closed to visitors)*, which is synonymous with the world of finance and the latest global financial crisis.

Take Pine Street to Chase Manhattan Plaza, the first skyscraper built in the *international style* of the 1960s, **then cross over Water Street on Maiden Lane,** which was flanked with bars and brothels in the 19th century. At the end of Maiden Lane, you will come to the pleasant historic ⑭ **South Street Seaport** district where you can end the day in style, perhaps at the Japanese restaurant **Suteishi** *(24 Peck Slip | tel. 1 212 7 66 23 44 | Budget–Moderate).*

4

THE BEST OF THE BEST

START: ① Rockefeller Center END: ⑭ Guggenheim Museum	5 hours Cycling/walking time (without stops) 2 hours
Distance: ⤵ 4.5 km/2.8 miles	
COSTS: Roosevelt Island Tram $5.50 (return), Citi-Bike rental bike $12/day, entrance fees $40, food $13	

From cultural highlights in the best museums in town and high-class shopping on Fifth Avenue and Madison Avenue to a bike ride through Central Park – this tour will show you New York at its finest.

① Rockefeller Center

10:00am Prometheus stands in the centre of Manhattan, surrounded by a huge office and shopping complex which a quarter of a million people walk through each day. Named after the man who commissioned them, John D. Rockefeller, the 14 buildings of ① **Rockefeller Center** → p. 45 **were built in 1929 between 48th and 51st**

Street on Fifth Avenue. The golden Prometheus sculpture is part of the decorative square beneath the Comcast Building → p. 45. **From here, take a little detour to the north to the venerable department store ❷ Saks Fifth Avenue** *(No. 611)* with its gigantic cosmetics department. Treat yourself to a little makeover by one of the make-up artists at the different counters.

With your freshly redone face, you'll be ready to tackle the big names in fashion – from Versace to Gap – **that line the sidewalks of Fifth Avenue, New York's famous shopping street. Go back to 55th Street and turn left to wander north down Madison Avenue. Walk through the lobby of the building ❸ 550 Madison Avenue** → p. 46, the former Sony Building. **Now head east to the ❹ Roosevelt Island Tramway** → p. 123 station. Drift `INSIDER TIP` over the East River in a cable car **before you return to the glamorous world of Fifth Avenue** – and the sparkling jewellery in the windows at **❺ Tiffany & Co.** → p. 79.

`01:00pm` **You should definitely wander through the ground floors of the upscale department store ❻ Bergdorf Goodman** → p. 76 to get a taste of this world-famous shopping world. If you've had your fill of busy stores, **unwind with a trip into the natural world of ❼ Central Park** → p. 50. Rent a bike from the inexpensive **❽ Citi Bike** → p. 129 system and cycle through the park. Hot dog stands are set up all around the park – grab one of these infamous New York fast food specialities for an impromptu picnic. There is a garden honouring The Beatles' John Lennon in the park at **72nd Street West before the Dakota Building** → p. 51 – the famous **❾ Strawberry Fields**.

`04:00pm` **After this little detour, head straight through the park to upper Fifth Avenue,** home to some of the most luxurious apartments in the city and some of the most interesting museums in the world. The **❿ Frick Collection** → p. 52 **on the corner of 70th Street** is housed in an elegant fin-de-siecle townhouse. The glass-covered atrium with its splashing fountain is an oasis of tranquillity! **Head back to ⓫ Madison Avenue** → p. 43. The street shows itself at its finest here with the boutiques of American and European designers. **When you get to 80th Street, walk back to Fifth Avenue, past the Metropolitan Museum of Art** → p. 53 with its huge

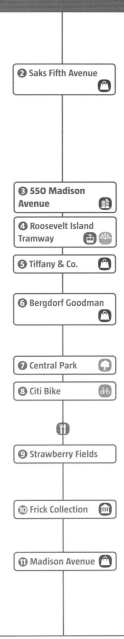

❷ Saks Fifth Avenue

❸ 550 Madison Avenue

❹ Roosevelt Island Tramway

❺ Tiffany & Co.

❻ Bergdorf Goodman

❼ Central Park

❽ Citi Bike

❾ Strawberry Fields

❿ Frick Collection

⓫ Madison Avenue

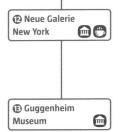

⑫ Neue Galerie
New York

⑬ Guggenheim
Museum

open staircase **towards 86th Street and the** ⑫ **Neue Galerie New York** → p. 54, which displays early 20th-century German and Austrian art. Top off a taste of exquisite art with a bit of Viennese coffee house flair in one of the cafés in the museum serving delicious apple strudel. It seems fitting to end the tour with an architectural highlight just **three blocks away,** namely the ⑬ **Guggenheim Museum** → p. 52, the great masterpiece of the architect Frank Lloyd Wright.

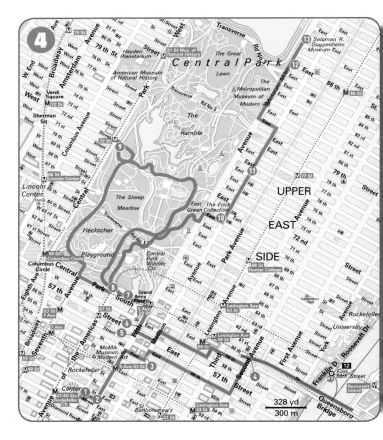

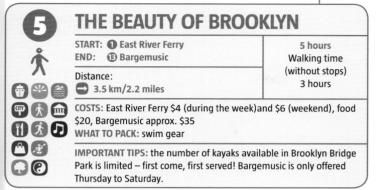

5 THE BEAUTY OF BROOKLYN

START: ❶ East River Ferry
END: ⓭ Bargemusic

5 hours
Walking time
(without stops)
3 hours

Distance:
➡ 3.5 km/2.2 miles

COSTS: East River Ferry $4 (during the week)and $6 (weekend), food $20, Bargemusic approx. $35
WHAT TO PACK: swim gear

IMPORTANT TIPS: the number of kayaks available in Brooklyn Bridge Park is limited – first come, first served! Bargemusic is only offered Thursday to Saturday.

Take a day trip to Brooklyn! Just a stone's throw away from Manhattan, you can walk through a huge park with lots of leisure activities and travel back in time in historic Brooklyn Heights.

`10:00am` The ❶ **East River Ferry** *(S Street | Pier 11 | www.eastriverferry.com)* **will bring you to** ❷ **Dumbo** → p. 56 where you can **enjoy a delicious breakfast at** ❸ **Café Almar** → p. 61. The former factory buildings and warehouses in this district that have been converted into apartments, offices, design shops and restaurants make this part of Brooklyn quite attractive. **Go inside** ❹ **Powerhouse** → **p. 74 on the corner of Water and Main Street,** a huge bookstore with changing photo exhibitions and frequent events. **Continue towards the water on Main Street until you come to** ❺ **Main Street Park** *(www.brooklynbridgepark.org)*. **At the little beach in the park,** enjoy the `INSIDER TIP` very best view of the Brooklyn Bridge with the skyline in the background! To the left-hand side, you will see a historic jewel housed in a glass pavilion, namely ❻ **Jane's Carousel** *(janescarousel.com)*, which was originally built in 1922. It costs just $2 to ride the horses on the carousel. It's now time for an absolutely lovely walk. **The recently developed** ❼ **Brooklyn Bridge Park** *(www.brooklynbridgepark.org)* **stretches along the East River to the south.** It has a lot to offer: gravel walkways climb over little hills and woodland copses while the pretty piers play host to sports such as basketball, boccia and beach volleyball to soccer or roller skating. Time for lunch? The restaurants at the beginning of Old Fulton Street are just a hop, skip and a jump to the west. Rent a kayak for free at the

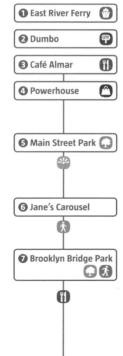

❶ East River Ferry

❷ Dumbo

❸ Café Almar

❹ Powerhouse

❺ Main Street Park

❻ Jane's Carousel

❼ Brooklyn Bridge Park

⑧ Brooklyn Bridge Park Boathouse

⑧ Brooklyn Bridge Park Boathouse *(June–Aug Sat 10am–3pm, Thu 5:30pm–6:45pm | Pier 2 | www.bbpboathouse.org)* and **explore New York from the water** – an unforgettable experience! **Back on land,** stretch out on the grass or swim a few laps in the pool to the tune of the seagulls and with a view of Manhattan and the Statue of Liberty.

⑨ Brooklyn Heights

⑩ River Deli

`02:00pm` **Then walk on and turn left down Joralemon Street. Go slightly uphill to get to the historic district of ⑨ Brooklyn Heights → p. 55. Right at the corner of Columbia Place, you will find the ⑩ River Deli** *(daily from 5pm | 32 Joralemon Street | tel. 1 718 2 54 92 00 | Expensive)*, a charming Italian restaurant. After a fine meal, **continue uphill and turn left on Hicks Street and left again on Remsen Street,** passing by elegant renovated brownstone houses shaded by trees. This picturesque part of Brooklyn was once home to many 20th-century American writers such as Truman Capote, Henry and Arthur Miller, Paul Bowles and Carson McCullers.

A slam dunk plus a skyline in Brooklyn Bridge Park

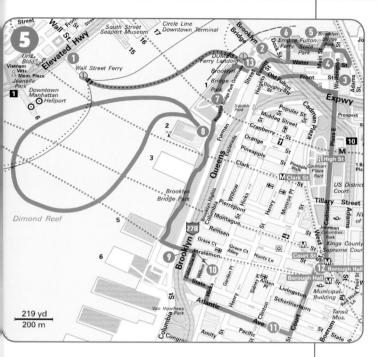

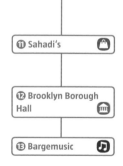

04:00pm **With no further delay, head to Atlantic Avenue.** This shopping street has many designer boutiques, antiques shops, restaurants and the popular Arabian deli ⑪ **Sahadi's** *(closed Sun | Atlantic Av. 187 | www.sahadis. com)* with all the charm of an old grocery store. Try some of the olives or INSIDER TIP one of the 150 different kinds of cheese! **Just half a block to the east, turn left on Court Street until you come to ⑫ Brooklyn Borough Hall**, the impressive former city hall of Brooklyn built in 1848. **Walk along Cadman Plaza Park for about 20 minutes to get back to the Brooklyn Bridge where a highlight in the form of a concert at ⑬ Bargemusic → p. 93** awaits – there is nothing quite like classical music in front of the gleaming backdrop of Manhattan.

⑪ Sahadi's

⑫ Brooklyn Borough Hall

⑬ Bargemusic

TRAVEL WITH KIDS

BRONX ZOO (159 E1) (⟋ 0)
Many of the more than 4,200 animals roam spacious outdoor enclosures. Next door is the *Botanical Garden. Tue–Sun 10am–6pm, end Oct–end March until 5pm | 2300 Southern Blvd./Corona Parkway | in Bronx Park | admission adults $33.95, children $23.95, Wed voluntary donation | www.bronxzoo.com | subway: 2 Pelham Parkway*

CHILDREN'S MUSEUM OF ARTS (143 D2) (⟋ D15)
Children under 15 can create their own works of art. *Mon–Wed noon–5pm, Thu, Fri noon–6pm, Sat/Sun 10am–5pm | 103 Charlton Street | admission $12 | tel. 1212 2 74 09 86 | www.cmany.org | subway: 1 Houston Street*

CHILDREN'S MUSEUM OF MANHATTAN (154 C5) (⟋ F2)
In a television studio children under 10 can make their own shows. *Tue–Sun 10am–5pm, Sat until 7pm | 212 W 83rd Street | admission $12 | tel. 1212 7 2112 23 | www.cmom.org | subway: 1 86 Street*

DISCOVERY ROOM (154 C6) (⟋ G3)
The American Museum of Natural History has an excellent interactive room where five to twelve year olds can touch and try out everything. *Sept–June Mon–Thu 1:30pm–5:10pm, Sat/Sun 10:30am–1:30pm, 2:15–5:10pm | 200 Central Park W/79th Street | admission adults $22, children $12.50 | www.amnh.org | subway: B, C 81 Street*

DYLAN'S CANDY BAR (152 B4) (⟋ H7)
Two floors of sweet delights. *1011 3rd Av./60th Street | tel. 1646 7 35 00 78 | www.dylanscandybar.com | subway: N, R, 4–6 Lexington Av./59 Street*

LEGO STORE (147 E4) (⟋ E11)
The huge Lego Store is a paradise for kids to play with building blocks – and parents to buy. *200 5th Av./23rd Street | stores. lego.com | subway: L, N, Q, R, 4, 5, 6, 14 Street-Union Square*

LULU'S CUTS & TOYS (158 C4) (⟋ 0)
It's a lively place, this colourful toyshop and hairdresser in Brooklyn's Park Slope. Every child can choose a video to watch while having a haircut, and lots of toys make the wait a fun time. *Daily | 48 Fifth Av. | tel. 1718 8 32 37 32 | luluskidscuts. nyc | subway: 2, 3, 4, 5 Atlantic Avenue/ Barclays Center*

Self-made animation films, exciting math tricks or a lesson in the trapeze school – New York fulfils every child's dream

MUSEUM OF MATHEMATICS
(147 E3) (*ECO E10*)

This museum features a number of fantasy-filled ways to teach children about mathematics with exhibits ranging from 3D creations to robots and mind games. *Daily 10am–5pm | 11 E 26th Street/5th Av. | admission adults $15, children $9 | www. momath.org | subway: 6 28 Street*

NEW YORK AQUARIUM (158 C5) (*ECO 0*)

Sharks, seals, penguins and baby otters make this outing to Coney Island interesting and cute. *Opening times depend on the season | 602 Surf Av./W 8th Street | Brooklyn | admission adults $11.95, children $15.95, online tickets often cheaper | www.nyaquarium.com | subway: F W 8 Street*

NEW YORK CITY FIRE MUSEUM
(142 C1) (*ECO B14*)

Put your helmet on and slide down the pole! This old fire department HQ is full of historic equipment: firemen's uniforms, tools and ancient-looking vehicles are a delight for kids. *Daily 10am–5pm | admission adults $8, children $5 | 278 Spring Street | www.nycfiremuseum.org | subway: 1 Houston Street*

ROOSEVELT ISLAND TRAMWAY
(152 C4) (*ECO H7*)

An aerial cableway rides every 15 minutes across the East River to Roosevelt Island. *Daily 6am–2pm | entrance: 59th Street and 2nd Av. | price $2.75 | www.rioc.ny. gov | subway: N, R, 4–6 Lexington Av./59 Street*

INSIDER TIP▶ TRAPEZE SCHOOL
(146 A6) (*ECO B13*)

Practice for children and adults. *Apr–Oct Mon–Thu from 10:30am, Fri, Sun from 8am, Sat from 9am | Hudson River Park, in line with Houston Street, on pier 40 | price (2-hour course, 10 pupils): $50–60, on weekends $70 | tel. 1 212 2 42 87 69 | www.newyork.trapezeschool.com | subway: A, C, E, 1 Canal Street*

FESTIVALS & EVENTS

You have at least three comprehensive weekly magazines to choose from to come to grips with the sheer volume of what's on offer – *New York, Time Out* and the free *Village Voice.* Another good option is the Weekend section of the *New York Times* on a Friday.

COMMEMORATION DAYS

The following are bank holidays when government offices are closed, but many shops offer sales for bargain hunters: **3rd Monday in Jan** *Martin Luther King's Birthday;* **3rd Monday in Feb** *Presidents' Day;* **2nd Monday in Oct** *Columbus Day;* **1st Tuesday in Nov** *Election Day;* **11 Nov** *Veterans Day*

EVENTS

JANUARY
Chinese New Year: ten-day festival with fireworks in Chinatown, between January and February

MARCH
On the 17th *St Patrick's Day*: procession of Americans with Irish roots on Fifth Avenue between 44th and 86th Street

APRIL
Easter Sunday: Easter Parade with costumes and outlandish hats on 5th Avenue in the vicinity of 48th to 57th Street
In the second half of the month, *TriBeCa Film Festival (www.tribecafilmfestival. com)*, hosted by Robert De Niro

JUNE
Museum Mile Festival: Fifth Avenue between 82nd and 104th Street with museum exhibitions, jugglers, clowns and musicians; The Metropolitan Opera offers exciting evening INSIDER TIP *open air concerts* in various parks free of charge
Gay and Lesbian Pride Day (Christopher Street Day) parade at the end of the month, Fifth Avenue

JULY
Independence Day: fireworks display on the East River or Hudson River at 9pm on 4 July. The best views are from FDR Drive or from West Side Highway but enquire about the actual launch site beforehand

SEPTEMBER
11 September: Commemoration of the victims of the 9/11 World Trade Center terror attacks in 2001

There is always something on – from cultural events like the TriBeCa Film Festival to the big parades on Halloween or Thanksgiving

Steuben Day Parade (*www.germanparade nyc.org*): A Fifth Avenue celebration by nationals of German origin honoring Prussian general Friedrich Wilhelm von Steuben, on a Saturday in the second half of September
In Mulberry Street south of Houston Street the ***Feast of San Gennaro*** (*www. sangennaro.org*) an annual market in honour of the patron saint of Naples runs for ten days mid-September
End of September to the beginning of October: ***New York Film Festival*** (*www. filmlinc.com*) held in the Museum of Modern Art and the Lincoln Center

OCTOBER
Halloween: celebrated on Sixth Avenue on the last day of the month by tens of thousands flaunting outlandish costumes to keep evil spirits at bay

NOVEMBER
New York Marathon (*www.ingnycmarathon. org*): first Sunday of the month. Starts at Verrazano Bridge and ends in Central Park

NATIONAL HOLIDAYS

1 Jan	New Year's Day
Last Mon in May	Memorial Day
4 July	Independence Day
First Mon in Sept	Labor Day
Fourth Thu in Nov	Thanksgiving
25 Dec	Christmas Day

Thanksgiving Day Parade: on the fourth Thursday this parade sets off from Central Park West and 77th Street to Macy's
At the end of November ***Rockefeller Christmas Tree Lighting*** (*www.rockefeller center.com*)

LINKS, BLOGS, APPS & MORE

LINKS & BLOGS

www.notfortourists.com *Not for tourists* publishes New York guidebooks that are full of tips even for New Yorkers. The website is also worth a visit!

www.theskint.com daily updates for free and cheap entertainment in the city

timeoutnewyork.com/things-to-do tips for shopping, exhibitions, readings, concerts and theatre

www.villagevoice.com the alternative newsweekly for hip, political New Yorkers

www.nycbloggers.com More than 6,000(!) bloggers contribute to this site. Sorted according to neighbourhood

en.wikipedia.org/wiki/List_of_songs_about_New_York_City Have you always wanted to know how many songs have been written about New York? Here is the (constantly growing) list

righterenyc.com Find out where Bob Dylan, Hemingway and Janis Joplin lived and take a walk around their neighbourhood

newyork.seriouseats.com Everything about food in New York – where to eat, the best desserts, beers, bagels and the latest food trends

blog.aptsandlofts.com Neely Wynn Moore is well connected and knows when new places open up

www.scoutingny.com A blog by a film location scout who spends his time looking for unique locations

mommypoppins.com Visiting the city with the kids in tow? This site will help you find the best things to do to keep the whole family entertained!

untappedcities.com/newyork This website is full of insider tips for New Yorkers and tourists alike

Regardless of whether you are still preparing your trip or already in New York: these addresses will provide you with more information, videos and networks to make your holiday even more enjoyable

freewilliamsburg.com The latest on what is happening in trendy Williamsburg: restaurant openings, events, local news and apartment listings

www.spottedbylocals.com/newyork Locals give tips on their hometown – that's the principle of *Spotted by Locals*. The New York Facebook page provides up to date recommendations from the community

theboweryboys.blogspot.com Two historians report on their podcast on New York and its history

VIDEOS & MUSIC

www.youtube.com/watch?v=j9jbdgZidu8 For many it's the best Christmas song: "Fairytale of New York" by The Pogues & Kirsty MacColl. The video was filmed in a police station on the Lower East Side

www.youtube.com/watch?v=xYIuX3b1NGE 3-minute documentary about the iconic Dakota building where many celebrities lived and where John Lennon was shot in 1980

short.travel/new2 This short film gives you a taste of the view from the observation deck at Rockefeller Center

short.travel/new9 When Ricky, the puppeteer, met the 86-year-old Doris on Washington Square, he modelled a marionette after her and then performed on the street. A warm-hearted short portrait of two New York originals

APPS

NYTimes The Scoop NYC Free iPhone app which has tips on where to shop, where to find the best cafés ("Filter") and outings ("Day Trips")

Goings On This free app from *The New Yorker* offers all sorts of cultural tips with insider knowledge about restaurants, concerts and exhibitions in New York

Explore 9/11 A memorial walking tour to the World Trade Center and the vicinity

Citi Bike The cheap bike rental option has an app with the same name that will help you find the nearest station – also tips for bike routes

TRAVEL TIPS

ARRIVAL

✈ Most flights from abroad arrive at *John F. Kennedy Airport (JFK)* in Queens. To book a *New York Airport Service* shuttle bus to Manhattan *(tel. 1 718 8 75 82 00 | www.nyairportservice. com)* go to the *Ground Transportation Center* at baggage claim *(every 20–30 min., travel time 60–75 min. | from $15)*. A taxi takes 60 to 75 min. to Manhattan and will charge you a $52 flat rate plus toll and a 15–20 per cent tip. The return journey to JFK by taxi is approx $50. Warning: only take the official taxis i.e. the yellow cabs. Other taxi drivers may offer you a cheaper ride but these are best avoided.

Your cheapest option will be the subway. Take the Airtrain *(travel time 12 min. $5 | www.panynj.gov)* in front of the terminal to the Howard Beach Station. Change trains and take the A train to Manhattan *(travel time approx. 1.5 hours | Metrocard $2.75)*. On the return journey only take the A trains in the direction of Far Rockaway/Mott Avenue or Rockaway Park Beach as far as the Howard Beach–JFK Airport Station. Or take the Airtrain to Jamaica Station ($5), change trains to the Long Island Rail Road *(travel time 35 min. | $9.50)* – congestion free until Penn Station and the perfect answer if your return flight falls during *rush hour*.

If your flight arrives at *Newark (EWR)* in New Jersey, take the Olympia Trails Bus to Midtown Manhattan *(every 15–20 min. travel time 60 min. | $16, return trip $28)*. Or take the Airtrain to NJ Transit or Amtrak, then head on to Penn Station *(travel time 45–60 min. | $13–15 | www. airtrainnewark.com)*. A taxi will take you about 60 min. and cost approx. $70 plus tip. A surcharge of $15 is applicable from New York.

National flights normally arrive at *La Guardia Airport (LGA)* in Queens. Bus: NY Airport Express *(travel time approx. 50 min. | $10)*. Express Shuttle *(travel time approx. 60 min. to Manhattan | $15)*. Taxi: 45 min., approx. $30 plus tip.

RESPONSIBLE TRAVEL

It doesn't take a lot to be environmentally friendly whilst travelling. Don't just think about your carbon footprint whilst flying to and from your holiday destination but also about how you can protect nature and culture abroad. As a tourist it is especially important to respect nature, look out for local products, cycle instead of driving, save water and much more. If you would like to find out more about eco-tourism please visit: *www.ecotourism.org*

CITY SIGHTSEEING TOURS

BY BOAT

A popular choice for tourists is the three-hour boat ride around Manhattan with ● *Circle Line Sightseeing Cruises* (150 B4) *(𝄞 C7)* *(mid-April–Oct daily 10am–3:30pm, in the winter once daily | pier 83 | W 42nd Street/Hudson River | price $42 | tel. 1212 5 63 32 00 | www.circleline42. com | subway: A, C, E 42 Street-Port Authority)*. The two-hour Brooklyn Circle Line Tour is completely new: for $38 you

From arrival to weather

get wind, waves and a New York cheese-cake called Little Fellas.

BY BUS

Gray Line New York (150 C5) (*Ⓜ E8*) *(Visitor Center: 42nd Street | Port Authority Bus Terminal's northern wing | between 8th and 9th Av. | tel. 1 800 6 69 00 51 | www.newyorksightseeing.com)* offers around 20 different tours – also to the surrounding area *(2–8 hours from $37)*, e.g. to Atlantic City or to the Hudson Valley. You can board the bus anywhere in the city.

Harlem Spirituals (151 D5) (*Ⓜ E8*) *(690 8th Avenue/between 43rd and 44th Street | tel. 1 212 3 91 09 00 | www.harlem spirituals.com | subway: A, C, E 42 Street-Port Authority)*: a tour through Harlem on Sunday mornings with a visit to a Baptist church *($75)*, Mon and Thu evenings *($175)* with a visit to a jazz club; two cocktails and dinner are included in the price.

BY AIR

Liberty Helicopters (142 B6) (*Ⓜ B18*) *(Pier 6, to the left of the Staten Island Ferry | tel. 1 212 9 67 64 64 | www.liberty helicopters.com | subway: N, R White-hall Street)*: 12–15 minute flips $199/person, 18–20 minutes $285/person, a private helicopter for five people for 18–20 minutes will cost $1,950. The prices are almost identical at *HeliNY (tel. 1 212 3 55 08 01 | heliny.com)* from the same pier.

BY BICYCLE

Bike the Big Apple (from $95, includes bicycle and helmet | tel. 1 347 878 98 09 | www.bikethebigapple.com): a range of

BUDGETING

Espresso	$2.50	for a shot at a stand-up bar
Hot dog	$2	for a hot dog
Cinema	from $12	for a ticket
Soft drink	$2.30	for bottled water/ Coca Cola
Taxi	$10	approx. for a short trip (2 miles)
Subway	$3	per ticket

tours through New York's different districts. The blue stations of *Citi Bike (www.citibikenyc.com)* are scattered all over New York. It costs $12 per day to use these bikes and $24 for three days, but there is a big catch: you have to park the bike every half hour at one of the many stations (and then you can take a new one right away). The system is only designed for short trips and errands, not for long tours.

DINNER CRUISES

World Yacht Cruises (150 B4) (*Ⓜ C7*) *(May–Dec daily, boarding at 6pm | pier 81, W 41st Street/Hudson River | dinner from $80 | tel. 1 212 6 30 81 00 | www.world yacht.com | subway: C, E 23 Street)* are not only a culinary delight but also a feast for the eyes as you watch the moon poised above the Statue of Liberty from your choice window seat.

CONSULATES & EMBASSIES

BRITISH CONSULATE GENERAL
845 3rd Av. | tel. 1 212 7 45 02 00 | www.ukinusa.fco.gov.uk | subway: 6 51 Street

CANADIAN CONSULATE
Mon–Fri 9–5pm | 1251 Avenue of the Americas | tel. 1 212 596 16 28 | can-am.gc.ca/new-york | subway: F 47–50 Street

IRISH CONSULATE GENERAL
345 Park Avenue, 17th Floor | tel. 1 212 319 25 55 | www.consulateofirelandnewyork.org | subway: 6 51 Street-Lexington Av.

CUSTOMS

The following goods can be imported duty-free into the USA: 1 litre of alcohol over 22 per cent, 200 cigarettes or 50 cigars or 2 kg tobacco and gifts up to a value of $100. Plants, fresh and tinned food may not be imported. The following goods can be imported duty-free into the EU: 1 litre of alcohol over 22 per cent or 2 litres of wine, 200 cigarettes or 250g of tobacco, 50g of perfume or 250g of eau de toilette and other goods (except gold) up to a value of £390/€430.

ELECTRICITY

110 Volt/60 Hertz. Small devices brought from Europe like hair dryers or shavers work with an adapter. Larger devices might require a transformer (available from electronics stores like Radio Shack). Otherwise charging can take a long time.

EMERGENCY

Free emergency number for police and medical assistance: 911.

EVENTS

For what's on, consult the *New York Times* (Fri, Sat). The *New York Post* and the *Daily News* publish a cinema programme daily. *New York Magazine* (Mon) lists cultural, sporting and other events. Also on Mondays *The New Yorker* gives an overview of what is on in the music and cinema scene, and much more. On Wednesdays, *Time Out* publishes the most comprehensive and current information on clubs and concerts i.e. music venues.

The free publication *Village Voice* gives weekly reviews and lists of cultural and political events. The best pre-selection of what is on makes its appearance at INSIDER TIP *www.flavorpill.com* on Tuesdays.

HEALTH

It is recommended that you take out travel health insurance when travelling to the United States. Accident and emergency departments (called emergency rooms, ER) are obliged to treat all patients, but they demand a credit card from non-US citizens.

The *Travelers Medical Center* (152 C2) (*m H4*) *(952 5th Av. | Suite 1D | tel. 1 212 7 37 12 12 | www.travelmd.com)* also comes highly recommended as a recognised 24-hour service and will also call on patients in their hotels.

IMMIGRATION

To travel to the United States you need a machine-readable passport with a digital chip containing biometric information, valid for the duration of your stay.

You must register online at least 72 hours before starting your journey *(https://esta.cbp.dhs.gov)* for an application. You are also obligated to fill out a form with your personal particulars before your trip. Your travel agency will be able to assist you with this. Among others the first address (hotel, vehicle hire point) where you will be staying has to be stated and there is a fee of $14.

The ESTA approval is valid for two years. Children must have their own passport, and for a stay longer than three months a visa is required.

INFORMATION

OFFICIAL NYC INFORMATION CENTER
(147 E4) *(ɰ E9)*

Information about everything from hotels to sightseeing tours. Also available here is the City Pass *(from $109 | www.newyorkpass.com)* which offers discounts, savings and other privileges and also means you can avoid long queues. They also sell tickets for basketball and football games, Broadway musicals and plays. *Mon–Fri 9am–7pm, Sat 10am–7pm, Sun 11am–7pm | 151 W 34th Street/7th Av. | tel. 1 212 4 84 12 22 | www.nycgo.com | subway: 1, 2, 3, A, C, E 34 Street-Penn Station*

BROOKLYN TOURISM COUNCIL
(139 E2) *(ɰ j21)*

Located in downtown Brooklyn, information and brochures on events, sightseeing and walking tours in Brooklyn, as well as on its history. *Mon–Fri 10am–6pm | 209 Joralemon Street | explorebk.com | subway: 2, 3, 4, 5 Borough Hall*

INTERNET

Go to *www.allny.com* for a good overview of informative websites. The websites of the city magazines *www.nymag.com* and *www.timeoutny.com* are also an excellent source, as is the *New Yorker* website: *www.newyorker.com.*

CURRENCY CONVERTER

$	£	£	$
1	0.77	1	1.29
3	2.32	3	3.88
5	3.87	5	6.46
13	10.05	13	16.40
40	30.94	40	51.70
75	58	75	97
120	93	120	155
250	193	250	323
500	387	500	647

For current exchange rates see www.xe.com

INTERNET ACCESS & WIFI

Instead of phone booths, the city has intalled 500 internet points with a free connection to the web. You can also charge up your mobile phone here.

You can surf the internet for free up to 30 minutes in all *public libraries*. Have the addresses of the libraries on you before you arrive: *www.nypl.org.*

Most parks, cafés and hotels offer free WiFi access. Caution: do not enter sensitive information such as passwords, etc. when logged on to these insecure networks!

MONEY, BANKS & CREDIT CARDS

1 dollar = 100 cents. *Bills* come in the following denominations: one, five, ten, 20, 50, 100 dollars. *Coins* in denominations of one, five, ten, 25, 50 cents and one dollar. Coins may also be referred to as follows: *penny* (1 cent), *nickel* (5 cents), *dime* (10 cents) and *quarter* (25 cents). The proverbial *buck* equals one dollar.

Credit cards are the most popular method of payment, especially Visa, MasterCard and American Express. You can also get money at a cash point (ATM) using a Debit Card with the Maestro logo (ATMs can be found at all banks and in many delis).

Make enquiries with your bank back home to find out whether it has an associated institution where you can draw money at no charge and whether your debit/credit card is valid in the United States. Most of the centrally located banks *(Mon–Fri 9am–3pm)* in New York have foreign exchange facilities, but these can often be expensive. On arrival be sure to have some cash and especially small denominations on you so you can pay your taxi, bus fare or porter. Taxi drivers are not obligated to give you change for notes higher than $20.

FOR BOOKWORMS AND FILM BUFFS

25th Hour – A drama by Spike Lee (2002) in which a convicted drug dealer roams the hot spots of New York with two friends contemplating his life ahead of serving a jail term

Gangs of New York – This epic film by Martin Scorsese (2002) takes you back to the New York of 1863. The streets are violent, its citizens volatile and there is the pervading threat of knife-bearing Bill the Butcher around every corner

Night at the Museum – At night when its visitors have deserted the building, the New York Museum of Natural History comes to life. Entertaining comedy (2006) starring Ben Stiller

New York Trilogy – Set against the backdrop of New York – a three-part sequel in which Paul Auster's protagonists go in search of themselves (1985–87) in the Big Apple

The Bonfire of the Vanities – In this satire on New York of the 1980s an arrogant investment broker inadvertently knocks down an African American male in the Bronx – and his world turns upside down. The film is based on the novel by Tom Wolfe (1987) starring Tom Hanks, Melanie Griffith and Bruce Willis

New York: The Novel – Edward Rutherfurd, the specialist for intriguing city portrait novels, covers 400 years of New York history in 880 pages (2011)

Extremely Loud and Incredibly Close – A film adaptation of Jonathan Safran Foer's novel narrated from the perspective of nine-year-old Oscar Schell who tries to follow in the footsteps of his father killed in the terror attack on the World Trade Center on 9/11 (2005). Film version (2011) with Tom Hanks and Sandra Bullock

Birdman – This black comedy with Michael Keaton and Emma Stone was an Oscar winner in 2014. In a fast-paced film by Alejandro Inarritu, an actor down on his luck races through New York to save his career

PHONE & MOBILE PHONE

Making a phone call works the same way as back home. A call from a phone booth costs approx. 50 cents. Details on how to make a call are shown on the phone device.

Dial 0 to get the operator, who can help with problems and to set up a return call (collect calls only within the United States).

Hotels charge at least $1 per minute and often add horrendous surcharges for long-distance calls so it pays to check before you dial.

In New York the area code always forms part of the phone number. For long-distance calls in the US: dial 1 before the area code (the numbers in this guide include the area and the long distance code); toll-free calls operate on the codes 800 and 888.

Code for calling overseas from the US: 011 followed by country code, e.g. UK 01144, Ireland 011353. Code for calling the US: 001.

Kiosks in New York sell prepaid cards ($5, $10 and $25). Some will make it possible to phone worldwide for as little as 3 cents/minute. You will be able to use these with your GSM tri-band or quad-band mobile phone, provided that your network operator is part of the international roaming agreement. But there may still be high roaming costs. Thus, it is also worth getting a prepaid SIM card for a local GSM network operator in the United States (Cellular One, T-Mobile USA, Verizon).

POST

The *General Post Office (8th Av./33rd Street)* is the only one that is open around the clock. Other post offices are generally open: *Mon–Fri 9am–5pm.*

Stamps are also available from the vending machines outside post offices or in some delis. The price of a stamp for a postcard to Europe is $1.20. Letterboxes are blue.

PUBLIC TOILETS

Public toilets or rest rooms are a scarce commodity in New York. With that said, atriums and lobbies accessible to the general public in a number of skyscrapers and shopping centres like Citicorp will have public toilets for visitors. Another alternative are the toilets located in the lobbies of big hotels, in department stores, in bookstores and in outlets of Starbucks and McDonald's.

PUBLIC TRANSPORT

BUS AND SUBWAY

The New York subway and bus network is seamless and will get you anywhere in the city. It is worth knowing that the NY subway express trains only stop at around every fifth station. Normal trains are called local trains. Some train stations have separate entrances for Uptown and Downtown trains.

The price for a single trip is $2.75. You can use it with a magnetic card, the *Metrocard*, which has a number of advantages: free transfers between the NY subway and buses, bulk discounts and a weekly ticket for $31 especially recommended for tourists.

The *Metrocard* is obtainable from NY subway stations, many kiosks and delis. You can also pay cash, $2.75 in coins, when catching a bus. Since the NY subway network is constantly being repaired expect detours and temporary suspensions – particularly on weekends. Information: *www.mta.info* or at the stations.

CAR HIRE

If you are planning to travel on from New York by car it is best to get your hire car at the airport. You get cheaper deals (from $50/day) than in Manhattan. Even more cost effective is to reserve your hire car before your trip.

Parking is a huge problem in Manhattan. There are too few parking spaces and the risk of break-ins and theft means that it is a better option to use parking garages (daily rates approx. $40).

For chauffeur-driven limos or town cars (from $85 per hour with a minimum of two hours plus 20 per cent tip and tax), call *Farrell Limousine Service (tel. 1 212 988 44 41)*.

TAXI

Authorised *yellow cabs* are not that expensive. The basic rate for the first third of a mile is $2.50, for every further fifth of a mile 50 cents. 25 blocks will cost you around $10 plus tip (15 per cent). A night surcharge of 50 cents applies from 8pm to 6am and on a weekday there is a $1 surcharge between 4pm and 8pm. Added to this is a bridge and tunnel toll.

Since 2013, green taxis have been operating on the streets of Brooklyn, Queens, Staten Island and the Bronx. You can only hail them in these boroughs.

You can call licensed taxi drivers through Uber using an app *(www.uber.com/de/cities/new-york)*. Leave the unmarked taxis to those who know their way around the city and are willing to haggle!

TICKETS

Telephonic reservations can be made via box offices but it is rare for most shows not to be sold out. Ticket services add a percentage surcharge to the ticket price and are available 24 hours: *Telecharge (tel. 1 212 2 39 62 00 | www.telecharge.com)* and *Ticketmaster (tel. 1 800 745 30 00 | www.ticketmaster.com)*.

Often hotel concierges will be able to assist you. Remember to tip them commensurate with services rendered. Half-price tickets for same day shows can be obtained from: *TKTS* (151 D5) *(m E7) (daily 3pm–8pm, tickets for matinees Wed and Sat 10am–2pm, Sun 11am–3pm | plus $2 service charge | Broadway/47th Street)*. Get them equally cheap without a waiting time at: *www.entertainment-link.com*.

TIME

New York is five hours ahead of London in the Eastern Standard Time (GMT – 5 hrs) zone. Daylight savings time is valid from the second Sunday in March until the first Sunday in November. NB: these dates do not coincide with when the UK changes its clocks.

TIPPING

In New York, tipping is not only welcomed, it is expected. European visitors should remember that in the United States tips are regarded as a part of the salary, not an added extra. Service staff need gratuities to earn a decent living. Your bill, or check, will include a tax of 8.875 per cent. New Yorkers simply multiply the tax by two and this is the figure they will give as a tip – 15 to 20 per cent. If you do not pay the exact amount of the bill, then you will get change. The tip is to be left on the table. If you pay with a credit card, then you write the amount of the tip on the line provided. Make sure to check the bill carefully because some restaurants fear that foreigners will not give a tip so they add their own gratuity – which means you don't need to leave a tip. Headwaiters and *maître de tables* in top class restaurants expect at least $10 for special favours like a window table, even as much as $20.

Hotel bellboys expect at least $1 per piece of baggage and at least $5 in the upscale ones. Chambermaids should get $5 at least and for longer stays $1 per day. Concierges providing special services (e.g. booking of show tickets or restaurant tables) should get at least a $10 tip. Taxi drivers expect a 15 per cent tip.

WEATHER, WHEN TO GO

New York's weather can be extreme. In winter it is often bitterly cold, in summer very humid, sometimes reaching temperatures of up to 104° F (40° C). It is a good idea to carry a light jacket around with you to avoid catching a cold when moving between air-conditioned interiors and the hot outdoors. The best time to go is from May to mid-June and mid-September to the end of October.

Temperatures will always be indicated in Fahrenheit (not Celsius) in the United States. To convert Celsius to Fahrenheit multiply the Celsius figure by 1.8 and add 32. 32° Fahrenheit equals 0° Celsius. Simple but not a rule of thumb: Fahrenheit minus 30, divided by two gives you Celsius.

50° F = 10° Celsius, 68° F = 20° Celsius
86° F = 30° Celsius, 95° F = 35° Celsius

WEATHER IN NEW YORK

	Jan	Feb	March	April	May	June	July	Aug	Sept	Oct	Nov	Dec
Daytime temperatures in °C/°F	4/39	5/41	9/48	14/57	21/70	25/77	28/82	27/81	24/75	18/64	12/54	6/43
Nighttime temperatures in °C/°F	-4/25	-4/25	0/32	5/41	11/52	17/63	19/66	19/66	16/61	10/50	4/39	-2/28
☀ Sunshine hours/day	4	6	7	8	8	10	9	8	8	6	5	4
☂ Precipitation days/month	8	7	9	9	8	7	7	7	6	5	8	8
≈ Water temperature in °C/°F	3/37	2/36	4/39	8/46	13/55	18/64	22/72	23/73	21/70	17/63	11/52	6/43

STREET ATLAS

The green line indicates the Discovery Tour "New York at a glance"
The blue line indicates the other Discovery Tours

All tours are also marked on the pull-out map

Exploring New York

The map on the back cover shows how the area has been sub-divided

Williamsburg

D · E · F

Rutledge
Wythe Ave
Heyward
Lynch
Lorimer
Walton
Walton
Ave
Bare
Whipple Ave
Throop

9
Flushing
Expwy
Wallabout
Street
Flushing Ave M
Hopkins St
St
Delmonico

Classon
Flushing
Franklin
Skillman
Bedford
Spencer
Walworth
Warsoff Pl
Nostrand
Marcy
Ellery
St
1

Park
Kent
Taaffe
Sandford
Marcy
Martin-Luther-King
Public School

Emerson
Ave
Place
Avenue
Myrtle
Avenue
Houses
Stockton
Ave
Avenue

Institute
Ave
Willoughby
Vernon
Myrtle
M
Myrtle
Willoughby Avs
Tompkins
2

Place
St
St
Hart
Marcy
Ave
G
Avenue

Lafayette
Houses
Ave
Kosciusko
Pulaski
Avenue

ON HILL M
Franklin
St
Avenue M
Lafayette
Pl
Herbert von King Park
Van Bu
3
Classon Ave
Beford
Nostrand Avs

Lexington
Ave
Avenue
Green
BEDFORD-STUYVESANT

B R O O K L Y N
St
Quincy
Ave
Gates
P
4
Quincy
Downing
Irving
St
Monroe
St
Madison
Ave
Putnam
High School

Putnam St
Jefferson
Hancock
St
Ave
Halsey
Arlington Pl
Macon
Verona
Id
MacDonough
Ave
n Avs
Claver Pl

berts
Public Library
Street
Fulton
M
Nostrad Ave
Street
5
P
Avenue
M
Franklin Ave
Place
Brevoort Pl
Herkimer
Avenue
Herkimer Pl

Ave
Ave
Bedford Pl
Ave
Atlantic
Ave
No.

St
Pacific
St
Dean
St
Bergen
Nursing & Rehabilitation Center
H
St
Saint Marks
6
M **Park Pl**
Rogers Ave
Nostrand
200 yd
250 m
C M

Pl
Prospect
Public School
Br

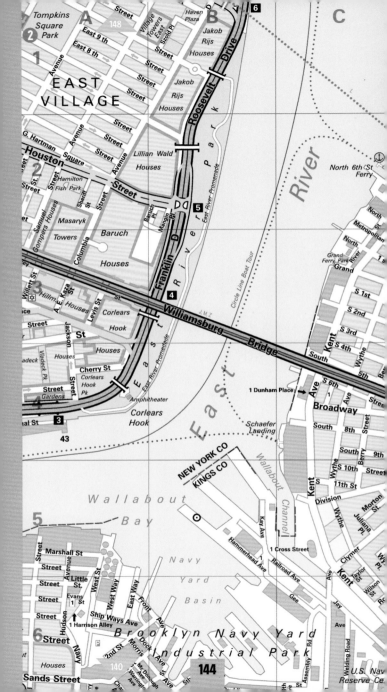

EAST VILLAGE

Tompkins Square Park

Village Towers East
148
East 9th
Street
East 8th
Street

Haven Plaza
Jakob Rijs Houses

Jakob Rijs Houses

Roosevelt Drive

A

B

C

G. Hartman Square
Houston
Street

Hamilton Fish Park

Lillian Wald Houses

East River Promenade

Park

River

North 6th St Ferry

Samuel Gompers Houses

Masaryk Towers

Baruch Houses

Columbia

5

North Metropolitan

North

Grand Ferry Park River

Grand

1 s

Willett St

Hillman St

A.E. Plaza St

Levis St

Corlears Hook

Jackson St

Houses

4

Williamsburg

J.M 7

Circle Line Boat Tour

Franklin

D River

E a s t

S 1st
S 2nd
S 3rd
S 4th

Kent

Wythe

5th

Vladeck Pk

Houses

Cherry St

Corlears Hook Pk

Street Gardens

Amphitheater

Corlears Hook

East River Promenade

Bridge

South

1 Dunham Place →

Ave

S 6th
Street

Broadway

3

nal St

43

Schaefer Landing

South

8th

South

9th

Wythe

S 10th

Street

Berry

NEW YORK CO

KINGS CO

Wallabout Channel

11th St

Division

Kent

Morton St.

Juliana Pl.

W a l l a b o u t

Bay

Marshall St

Street

Street

Little St.

West St

Evans 1 St

Street

Hudson

Ship Ways Ave

1 Harrison Alley

Navy

Yard

Basin

Kay Ave

Hammerhead Ave

Railroad Ave

1 Cross Street

Gee

West Way

East Way

Front

Dock

2nd St

McDonough

Warrington

B r o o k l y n N a v y Y a r d

I n d u s t r i a l P a r k

140

Morris

Assembly Rd

Clymer

Taylor St

Wilson St

Jay

Ave

Welding Road

U.S. Nav Reserve Ce

144

6
Street

Houses

Sands Street

he House
J.S. General Post Office

D

33 rd
35 th
36 th
American Standard Bldg.
Public Library
151

East
East
Library
Lincoln Bldg.
Bowery Bank

M 34 St Penn Station
Nelson Tower
DISTRICT
East
East

East
East

East

Madison Square Garden
1 Penn Plaza
M 34 St Penn Station
Macy's
Herald Square
8
MURRAY

Pennsylvania RR Station
2 Penn Plaza
34 St Herald Sq
34 th
Street
Morgan Library & Museum

31 st
West
33rd St (PATH)
Greeley Square
Street
Fifth Avenue

30 th
29 th
St.John
St. Francis of Assisi
Empire St.Bldg.
Church of the Incarnation
HIL

HATTAN
St.John
32-nd
Street
East
35 th
36 th

Fashion Institute of Technology
27 th
26 th
25 th
th
SJM-Bldg.
28 th
Marble Collegiate Reformed Church
M 28 St
Street
East
East-
Avenue
Avenue
South
M 33 St

ea tel
M 23 St
23 rd
23rd St (PATH)
Saint Sava
Street
Street
Broadway
Street
Street
Street
Little Church around the Corner
East
33-rd
32-nd
31st
30th
29 th
2

1
Americas
Street
Street
N.Y. Life Insurance Company Appellate Court of N.Y.
Curry Hill
Avenue
Third Avenue

FLATIRON
M 23 St
Street
Worth Mon.
Madison Square Park
M 23 St
Flatiron Bldg.
East
Metropolitan Life Insurance Comp.
27 th
26 th
25 th
69th Reg. Armory
Street
Street
3

DISTRICT
of "Fashion Row"
The
Street
East
24 th
B.M.Baruch College
23 rd
East Midtown Plaza
Phipps

useum
Th. Roosevelt Birthplace
St Francis Xavier Academy
Broadway
East
Gramercy Pk West
Gramercy Pk 21 st
22 nd
Street
Peter
Second Avenue

14th St (PATH)
M
Street
East
Park
Nat'l Arts Club
20 th
19 th
GRAMERCY
Police Academy Mus.
Street
4

4 St
School for Social esearch
Street
East
Union Sq.W.
Union Sq Park
18 th
17 th
Cabrini Medical Center
Avenue

ry)
Forbes Bldg.
Church of the Ascension
Fifth
East
East
14 St Union Sq
M
16 th
15 th
Consolidated Edison Bldg.
Hospital for Joint Diseases
Peter

N.Y.U.
versity Place
Broadway
Union Sq E
14 th
13 th
St George's Episcopal
3 Ave
Stuyvesant Sq
Beth Israel Medical Center

ENWICH
Mark Twain's House
Wash. Ms.
Fourth Avenue
Grace Church
12 th
11 th
10 th
First Avenue
Loop
Stuyvesant
5

VILLAGE
Uni-
Greene
E 8th
Third Avenue
American Theatre
M 1 Ave

Wash Sq
Waverly Pl
9 th
St. Mark's in the Bowery Church
H

N.Y. University
Washington Pl
M Astor Pl
Astor Pl
A
ALPHABET

ton
4 th Pl
University Pl
8 St NYU
Cooper Union
Stuyvesant St Marks
Street

Universal Jazz Coalition
Merchants House Mus.
Public Th.
Cooper Square
St Marks Pl
Ukrainian Museum
CITY
6

Broadway
Bond
Bayard Condict Bldg.
Great
Jones St
East
First
2
Tompkins

Broadway-Lafayette St
Street
Bowery
Second
147
7 th
6 th
143
Square
Park
East 9th

D

E

F

Library
Consolid. Edison
Learning Center

Blvd

43 rd St

Street

43 rd Street

Queens Plaza

22 nd

23 rd

153

Vernon
9 th

11 th
Road

12 th
Street

44 th

13 th
Street

Street

Silvercup
Studios

42 nd
Street

Dutch
Kills

22 nd
Road

M

44 th

5 th St

44 th
44 th

10 th
Street

21 st

23 rd

Crescent

Hunter

Avenue

24 th

45 th

North Basin
Rd

Blvd

QUEENS

45 th

Avenue

Road

Court Sq
23 St

Drive

M

Court Sq

M

Pepsi
Sign

46 th

Street

46 th

Street

45 th

Road

Ave

P.S.1
Contemp.
Art Center
& Museum

M

21 st

Thomson Ave

2

Gantry
Plaza
State

47 th

47 th

Street

46 th

Road

21th

Avenue

M

21 St

Davis St

Court
House

Crane St

Court Sq

Pearson St

Five Pointz
(demolished)

Hunter

Purves St

48 th

Avenue

Road

Center

Hunters Point

50 th

Chocolate Factory
Theater

Vernon

11th

Avenue

Hunters
Pt. Station

Skillman

47 th

Pearson

3

5 th
Avenue

Ave

Jackson

Vernon Blvd
Jackson Ave

M

49 th

Avenue

M

Hunters Point Ave

50th

Avenue

27th

Avenue

Dutch

den

Avenue

Toll

Long Island

Long Island
City-station

Avenue

Pulaski Bridge

11th St

51st

23rd St

25th St

Ave

Ave

495

Ash St

Newton

29th

Railroad

4

Street
Box

Street

Paidge
St

Ave

Provost

Creek

Clay

Street

Street

Manhattan

Dupont

Street

Street

Commercial

Franklin

McGuinness

Street

Street

Street

Kingsland
Av

Newtown Creek
Water Pollution
Control Plant

5

Street

Greenpoint Avenue

Kingsland

Greenpoint Ave

M

Blvd

Avenue

Humboldt

Russel

Monitor

North

Street

McGuinness

Jewel

Diamond

Moultrie

Greenpoint

Street

Newel

Calyer

Street

Eckford

Avenue

Henry

Street

Leonard

200 yd

250 m

6

Sutton

Street

Clifford
Pl

Guernsey

Lorimer

Norman

Street

Bankers

Dobbin

Street

St

Meserole

149

145

Nassau

WEEHAWKEN

A   **B**   **C**

River

Park

South

Dimaggio

Joe

1

200 yd

250 m

Weehawken
Port Imperial

2

99

98

96

West
Power
Plant

VIA-57 West

West

HUDSON CO

NEW YORK CO

NEW JERSEY

NEW YORK

Twelfth Avenue

8

West

94

Clinton
Cove Park

West

West

Show
Piers

DeWitt
Clinton
Park

West

AT&T

3

92

90

Manhattan Cruise
Terminal

West

Avenue

West

Women's
Int.
Arts Center

88

West

West

Irish Arts
Ctr. Theater

86

West

West

C

N.
of

84

Intrepid
Sea-Air-Space
Museum

West

West

Twelfth

4

CIRCLE LINE BOAT TOUR

Pier 83

Circle Line Cruises

West

West

P

World Financial Center
Pier 11/Wall St

CIRCLE LINE BOAT TOUR

81

World
Yacht

West

Avenue

West

1

P HELLS
KITCHEN

St. C

Lincoln Tunnel (Toll)

West Midtown
Ferry

West

79

West

Silver
Towers

West Side
Theaters

Lincoln Harbour

76

78

West

West

St Raphael

5

P

42 St Port Aut
Bus Ter

Penn-
Central
Tunnel

9a

J.K.Javits
Exhibition and
Convention
Center of
New York

West

West

St. Raphael

Theater
Complex

Holy
Cross C

Manhattan Plaza

Port Author
Bus Termin

Dimaggio

West

Seventh

M 34 St-
Hudson Yards

YMCA-
Sloane House

34th

6

West 30 St
Heliport

Hudson Yards
(under constr. 2025)

Office &
Residential

55

Retails
Pavilion

The
Shed

Schools

Retails · Shops ·
Restaurants

Vessel

50

Tenth

33rd

Ninth

37th

35th

West

West

146

West

150

10

33rd

U.S. General

Eighth

Ave

M 34 St
Penn Station

Nels

Streets and Avenues (north area):
- Rutgers
- West Verdi Square
- 74 th St
- 73 rd Street
- 72 nd
- 71 st
- 70 th
- 69 th
- 68 th
- 67 th
- Riverside
- Freedom Pl
- Lincoln Towers
- Sherman Sq
- M 72 St
- N.Y. Hist. Society
- 154
- Bank Rock Brid
- The Lake
- Bow Bridge
- The Dakota
- M 72 St
- Strawberry Fields
- Cherry Hill Fountain
- Bethesda Terrace

Central area:
- Red Cross
- Con-Edison
- Stev's Towers
- A. Tully Hall
- Hearst Plaza
- IMAX-Theatre
- 66 St Lincoln Center
- Amerik. Folk Art Museum
- Bowling and Cricket Fields
- Naumburg Bandshell
- The Sheep Meadow
- Amsterdam Houses
- Metropolitan Opera
- Guggenheim Bandshell
- Damrosch Pk.
- Big Apple Circus
- N.Y.State Theater
- Vivian Beaumont Th.
- Avery Fisher Hall
- Dante pl.
- Lincoln Plaza
- 65 Street
- 64 Street
- Tavern on the Green
- Heckscher
- Coll. of Justice
- Mount Sinai Roosevelt Hospital
- St. Paul Street
- Fordham University
- Publlibrary Art Mus.
- YMCA-West-Side
- Century Apartm.
- Carousel
- Chess and Checkers
- Children's Zoo
- Coliseum Pk.
- Time Warner Ctr.
- Trump International Hotel & Tower
- Playground
- The Dairy
- Central Park Wildlife Ctr.
- 59 St Columbus Circle
- Wollman Rink
- The Arsenal
- Columbus Circle
- Museum of Arts and Design
- Gapstow Bridge
- Nature Sanctuary
- The Pond

Midtown:
- Alvin Ailey Dance Theatre
- St. George
- Fine Arts Bldg.
- Athletic Club
- W Arts Bldg.
- Arlen
- MONY Tower
- Cami Hall
- 58 th
- St.Clare's Hosp.
- St. Benedict
- Carnegie Hall
- Metrop. Tower
- Russian Tea Room
- J.B.Zankel Hall
- Grand Army Plaza
- Hotel Pierre
- Getty Bld
- 57 St 7 Ave
- 1700 Bway
- Alliance Capital Man.
- Plaza Hotel
- 5 Ave 59 St
- Financial Corp.Bldg.
- Gen. Motors Bldg.
- 7th Ave Bldg.
- 7 Ave
- Solow Bldg.
- Squibb Bldg.
- MGM Bldg.
- Medical Arts Hosp.
- Tiffany
- Trump Tower
- Standard Brands Bldg.
- Worldwide Plaza
- Param. Plaza
- Sheraton Hilton
- N.Y. Convention & Visitors Bureau
- Credit Lyonnais Bldg.
- ITT Bldg.
- 5th Ave Presb. Church
- MoMA Museum of Modern Art
- St. Thomas
- IBM Bldg.
- Glass Bldg.
- Fuller Bldg.
- Sony Bldg.
- Equitable Center
- P. Webber
- CBS Bldg.
- Sperry Rand Bldg.
- Museum of TV and Radio
- Time&Life Bldg.
- Exxon Bldg.
- Radio City Music Hall
- GE Bldg.
- Internat'l Bldg.
- Tishman Bldg.
- 5 Ave/53 St
- Lever House
- Park Ave Plaza
- Citibank Bldg.
- Seagram Bldg.
- THEATER DISTRICT
- Duffy Sq
- N.Y. Marriott Marquis
- TKTS
- McGraw Hill Bldg.
- 1211 Ave of the Americas
- Rockefeller Center
- 47-50 Sts Rockefeller Ctr
- Olympic Tower
- St. Patrick's Cathedral
- 345 Park Av.
- Viacom Bldg.
- N.Y. Times Bldg.
- Paramount Bldg.
- ABC Bldg.
- Stevens Tower
- Americas Tower
- 1166 Ave of the Americas
- (Diamond Row)
- Dahesh Mus.
- Helmsley Palace
- Tower 49
- Bartholomew's
- St. Bart's Bldg.
- G.S.M. Bldg.
- 51 St
- Times Square
- Madame Tussaud's
- Times Sq 42 St
- Int. Center of Photography
- 1133
- 1155
- MIDTOWN
- 270 Park Ave Bldg.
- Fred F French Bldg.
- The Waldorf-Astoria
- Westrace
- Chem. Bank Bldg.
- American Brands Bldg.
- 49
- Verizon
- 42 St Bryant Pk
- Grace Bldg.
- Bank of N.Y. Bldg.
- Helmsley Bldg.
- 48 th
- Lewisohn Bldg.
- 5 Ave
- Met Life Bldg.
- YMCA Vanderbilt
- American Standard Bldg.
- Bryant Park
- N.Y. Public Library
- Grand Central Terminal
- St. Agnes
- 151
- 147
- Grand Central 42 St
- Hyatt N.Y.
- Seventh Avenue
- Broadway
- Amsterdam Avenue
- Columbus Avenue
- Central Park West
- Central Park South
- Fifth Avenue
- Madison
- Park Ave
- Vanderbilt

Grid labels: D, E (top); 1, 2, 3, 4, 5, 6 (right side); star markers numbered 15, 14; circled numbers 1, 2, 3, 4, 5, 6, 7, 8, 9, 10.

EDGEWATER

A   **B**   **C**

1

200 yd
250 m

2

BERGEN CO
HUDSON CO
NEW JERSEY
NEW YORK
NEW YORK CO

Circle Line Boat Tour

11

3

West
Riverside West
West
West
West

Soldiers & Sailors Monument

Riverside

West
Riverside Drive
93 rd

Amsterdam

91 st

West Riverside

9a

West Drive
90 th

4

Riverside Park

Hudson Drive

West
& West End
West
Historical

B'nai Jeshurun

89 th

88 th

West
Riverside
West
Amsterdam
West
Houses

District

M **86 St**

87 th

86 th

Jewis

SID

5

79th Street
Boat Basin

10

West End
Broadway

Childrens
Museum
of Manhattan

84 th (Edgar Allen Poe S

85 th

H 83 rd

82 nd

Jesus Christ R.

81 st

First Baptist
Church

M **79 St**

80 th

Hayden
Planetarium
Rose Ctr. for
Earth & Space

79 th St.

78 th St

6

9

Henry

Riverside

West

West
West

West
West

Eleanor
Roosevelt
Monument

West

West 72 nd St

Ansonia
Hotel

Rutgers

Highway Blvd

Riverside
Ide

West

151

154

77 th
76 th Green
Flea Market

75 th

74 th

73

American Museum
of Natural History

Street

N.Y. Hist.
Society

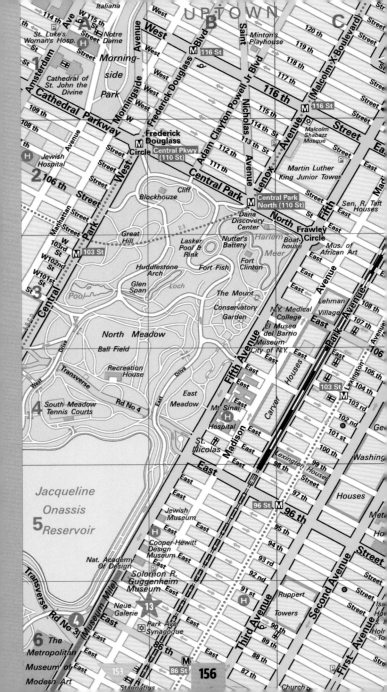

A B C

Italiana
West

Saint

Minton's
Playhouse

120 th Street

114 th Ave
th A B 115

St. Luke's
Woman's Hosp.

Street Notre
Dame

West Avenue

119 th Street

116 St

118 th Street

Cathedral of
St. John the Divine

Morning-
side

West

Frederick Douglass

Nicholas

Jr Blvd

Adam Clayton Powell

117 th Street

116 th Street

116 St

Cathedral Parkway

Park

West

West

115 th St

114 th St

Malcolm Shabazz
Mosque

Malcolm X Boulevard

Street

East

109 th

Morningside

West

Frederick
Douglass
Circle

113 th St

Avenue

Street

108 th

Jewish
Hospital

Manhattan

Avenue

Street

Street

Central Pkwy
(110 St)

112 th

111 th Street

Lenox

Avenue

Martin Luther
King Junior Tower

Fifth

Sen. R. Taft
Houses

106 th Street

West

Park

Central Park

Cliff
Blockhouse

Central Park
North (110 St)

North

Harlem

Boat-
house

Frawley
Circle

Mus. of
African Art

103rd
St

W103rd
St

103 St

Great
Hill

Dana
Discovery
Center

Nutter's
Battery

Meer

East

Avenue

East

Lehman
Village

108 th

W102nd
St

Huddlestone
Arch

Lasker
Pool &
Rink

Fort Fish

Fort
Clinton

East

107 th

W101st
St

Central

Glen
Span

Loch

The Mount

Conservatory
Garden

N.Y. Medical
College

Park

East

106

Lexington

Avenue

105 th

Pool

North Meadow

El Museo
del Barrio
Museum

City of N.Y.

East

East

103 St

104 th

103 rd

Ball Field

East

Fifth Avenue

East

Houses

East

102 nd

Transverse

Recreation
House

Carver

101 st

South Meadow
Tennis Courts

Road No 4

East
Meadow

Mt Sinai
Hospital

East

East

100 th

Lexington Houses

99 th Street

Dr

St.
Nicolas

Madison

East

98 th

East

97 th

East

Jacqueline

East

96 St

96 th

Houses

Met

Onassis

Jewish
Museum

East

95 th

Reservoir

Cooper-Hewitt
Design
Museum

East

94 th

Nat. Academy
Of Design

East

93 rd

Solomon R.
Guggenheim
Museum

East

92 nd

Second Avenue

Street

Neue
Galerie

East

91 st

Ruppert

Third Avenue

Street

13

East

Towers

90 th

Park Ave
Synagogue

East

89 th

Transverse

Rd No 3

East

East

88 th

First Avenue

The
Metropolitan
Museum
Modern Art

East

86 St

86 th

87 th

Church

Street

Museum Mile

Staanatius

153

156

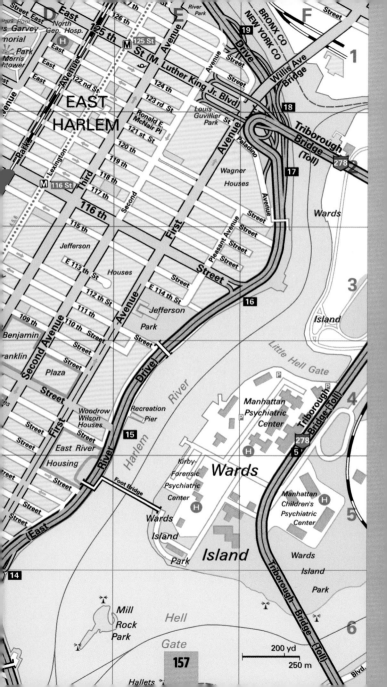

This index lists a selection of the streets and squares shown in the street atlas

1..9

1st Place (Brooklyn) **139/D5**
1st Place (Manhattan) **142/A5**
1st Street **139/F6-E5**
2nd Place **142/A5**
2nd Place (Brooklyn) **139/D5-F6-140/A1-144/A6**
2nd Street (Queens) **149/D4**
3rd Avenue **139/E6**
3rd Place (Brooklyn) **138/C5**
3rd Place (Manhattan) **142/A5**
3rd Street **139/F6-D5**
4th Avenue **139/F6**
4th Place **138/C5**
5th Street (Brooklyn) **140/B1**
5th Street (Queens) **149/D2-D3**
6th Avenue **140/A6**
6th Street **139/E6**
7th Avenue **140/B6**
7th Street **139/E6**
9th Street (Brooklyn) **139/D6**
9th Street (Queens) **149/E1-153/F5**
10th Street **149/E1-149/E6**
11th Street **149/E1-E3-153/F5**
12th Street **149/E1-153/F6**
13th Street **149/E1-153/F6**
21st Street **149/F1**
22nd Street **149/F1-153/F6**
23rd Street **149/F1-E3-F2**
24th Street **149/F1-F2**
27th Street **149/F3**
29th Street **149/F4**
35th Avenue **153/F4**
36th Avenue **153/F4**
37th Avenue **153/F5**
38th Avenue **153/F5**
40th Avenue **153/F5**
41st Avenue **153/F6**
42nd Road **149/F1**
43rd Avenue **149/E1**
44th Avenue **149/E1**
44th Drive **149/D1**
44th Road **149/E1**
44th Street **149/F2**
45th Avenue **149/D2**
45th Road **149/E2**
46th Avenue **149/D2**
46th Road **149/D2**
47th Avenue **149/F3-D2**
47th Road **149/D2**
48th Avenue **149/D2**
49th Avenue (Hunters Point Ave) **149/E3**
50th Avenue **149/D3-F3**
51st Avenue **149/D3-E3**
53rd Avenue **148/C3**
54th Avenue **148/C3**

A

Abraham E. Kazan Street **143/F3-144/A3**
Adam Clayton Powell Junior Boulevard **155/F2-156/B2**
Adams Street **139/E2**
Ainslie Street **145/E4**
Albany Street **142/A4**
Allen Street **142/E3**
Amsterdam Avenue **151/D3-154/C4-155/D3-156/A1**
Ann Street **142/B4**
Arch Street **149/E2**

Ashland Place **140/A2**
Ash Street **149/D4**
Assembly Road **140/C1**
Astor Place **147/D5**
Atlantic Avenue **139/D3-140/B4-141/E5**
Attorney Street **143/F2**
Avenue A **143/F1**
Avenue B **143/F1-144/A1**
Avenue C **144/A2**
Avenue D **144/A2**
Avenue of the Americas **147/E1-151/D6**
Avenue of the Finest **142/C4**

B

Banker Street **149/D6**
Bank Street **146/B4**
Barclay Street **142/B3**
Barrow Street **146/B5**
Battery Place **142/A5**
Baxter Street **143/D3**
Bayard Street **143/D3**
Beach Street **142/B2**
Beaver Street **142/B5**
Bedford Avenue **141/D1-144/C5-145/D4**
Bedford Street **146/B5**
Beekman Street **142/C4**
Berkley Place **140/A6**
Berry Street **144/C4**
Bethune Street **146/B4**
Bleecker Street **146/C6-B4**
Bloomfield Street **146/A3**
Boerum Place **139/E3**
Bond Street **147/D6**
Borden Avenue **149/D3**
Bowery **143/D3-E1-147/D6**
Box Street **149/D4**
Bridge Street (Brooklyn) **143/F5**
Bridge Street (Manhattan) **142/A6**
Broad Street **142/B6**
Broadway **142/B5-143/D1-147/D5-154/B5-155/D3**
Brooklyn Bridge **143/D5**
Brooklyn Queens Expressway **138/C5-139/F1-140/A1-143/D6**
Broome Street **142/C1-143/E2**

C

Cadman Plaza West **139/E1-143/E6**
Calyer Street **145/D1-148/C6-149/E6**
Canal Street **142/B1-143/E3-146/A6**
Carlisle Street **142/A4**
Cathedral Parkway **155/D1**
Cathedral Place **139/F1**
Catherine Street **143/D4**
Cedar Street **142/B4-B5**
Center Street **143/D3**
Central Park North **155/F2-156/B2**
Central Park South **151/E3**
Central Park West **151/E2-152/A2**
Centre Market Place **143/D2**
Chambers Street **142/A2**
Charles Street **146/B5**
Charlton Street **146/B6**
Chatham Square **143/D3**

Cherry Street **143/E4-144/A4**
Christopher Street **146/B5**
Chrystie Street **143/D3**
Church Street **142/B3**
Clarkson Street **146/B6**
Classon Avenue **141/D1**
Clay Street **149/D4**
Cleveland Place **143/D2**
Clifford Place **149/D6**
Cliff Street **142/C5**
Clinton Street **143/F3-F4**
Clymer Street **144/C5**
Collister Street **142/B2**
Columbia Heights **139/D2**
Columbia Street (Brooklyn) **138/C4**
Columbia Street (Manhattan) **144/A3**
Columbus Avenue **151/D3-155/D3-D4**
Columbus Circle **151/E3**
Commercial Street **149/D4**
Congress Street **139/D3**
Conselyea Street **145/E3**
Cornelia Street **146/C5**
Cortlandt Avenue **142/C3**
Court Square **149/F2**
Court Street **139/D4-E3**
Cranberry Street **139/D1-143/D6**
Crane Street **149/F2**
Crescent Street **149/F2**
Crosby Street **143/D2**

D

Davis Court **149/F3**
Davis Street **149/F2**
Dekalb Avenue **140/A3-C3**
Delancey Street **143/F3-E2**
Desbrosses Street **142/B1**
Diamond Street **149/E5**
Division Avenue **144/C5**
Division Street **143/E3**
Dobbin Street **145/E1-149/D6**
Dock Street **143/E5**
Dominick Street **142/B1**
Doughty Street **143/E6**
Dover Street **143/E5**
Downing Street **146/B6**
Driggs Avenue **145/D5**
Duane Street **142/B3**
Dupont Street **149/D4**
Dutch Street **142/B4**

E

Eagle Street **148/C5**
Earlybird Road **138/A3**
East 1st Street **143/E1**
East 2nd Street **143/E1**
East 3rd Street **143/E1-147/D6**
East 4th Street **147/D6**
East 5th Street **147/E6**
East 6th Street **147/E6**
East 7th Street **147/E6**
East 8th Street **144/A1-147/D5**
East 9th Street **144/A1-147/F6-D5**
East 10th Street **147/D5**
East 11th Street **147/D5**
East 12th Street **147/D5**
East 13th Street **147/D4**
East 14th Street **147/D4**
East 15th Street **147/D4-148/A6**
East 16th Street **147/D4-148/A6**

East 17th Street **147/D4**
East 18th Street **147/D4**
East 19th Street **147/D4**
East 20th Street **147/E3**
East 21st Street **147/E3**
East 22nd Street **147/E3**
East 23rd Street **147/E3**
East 24th Street **147/E3**
East 25th Street **147/E3**
East 26th Street **147/E3**
East 27th Street **147/E3**
East 28th Street **147/E2**
East 29th Street **147/E2**
East 30th Street **147/E2**
East 31st Street **147/E2**
East 32nd Street **147/E2**
East 33rd Street **147/E2**
East 34th Street **147/D1**
East 35th Street **147/F1**
East 36th Street **147/F1**
East 37th Street **147/F1**
East 38th Street **147/F1**
East 39th Street **147/F1**
East 40th Street **147/F1**
East 41st Street **147/F1**
East 42nd Street **147/F1-148/A1**
East 43rd Street **151/E6**
East 44th Street **151/E6**
East 45th Street **151/E6**
East 46th Street **151/E6-152/A6**
East 47th Street **151/F6-152/B6**
East 48th Street **151/E5-152/A5**
East 49th Street **151/E5-152/A5**
East 50th Street **151/E5-152/A5**
East 51st Street **151/F5-152/A5**
East 52nd Street **151/F5-152/A5**
East 53rd Street **151/F5-152/A5**
East 54th Street **151/F5-152/B5**
East 55th Street **151/F4-152/A4**
East 56th Street **151/F4-152/A4**
East 57th Street **151/F4-152/B4**
East 58th Street **151/F4-152/A4**
East 59th Street **152/B4**
East 60th Street **151/F4-152/A4**
East 61st Street **152/B4**
East 62nd Street **151/F3-152/B3**
East 63rd Street **152/B4**
East 64th Street **152/B3**
East 65th Street **152/B3**
East 66th Street **152/B3**
East 67th Street **152/B3**
East 68th Street **152/B3**
East 69th Street **152/B3**
East 70th Street **152/B2**
East 71st Street **152/C2**
East 72nd Street **152/B2**
East 73rd Street **152/B2**
East 74th Street **152/B2**
East 75th Street **152/C2**
East 76th Street **152/C2**
East 77th Street **152/C1**
East 78th Street **152/C1**
East 79th Street **152/C1**
East 80th Street **152/C1**
East 81st Street **152/C1**
East 82nd Street **152/C1**
East 83rd Street **152/C1-155/E6-156/A6**
East 84th Street **155/E6-156/A6**
East 85th Street **155/E6-156/A6**
East 86th Street **153/D1-155/E6-156/A6**

East 87th Street **155/F6-156/B6**
East 88th Street **155/F6-156/B6**
East 89th Street **155/F6-156/B6**
East 90th Street **155/F5-156/B5**
East 91st Street **155/F5-156/B5**
East 92nd Street **155/F5-156/B5**
East 93rd Street **155/F5-156/B5**
East 94th Street **155/F5-156/B5**
East 95th Street **155/F5-156/B5**
East 96th Street **155/F5-156/B5**
East 97th Street **155/F4-156/B4**
East 98th Street **155/F4-156/B4**
East 99th Street **155/F4-156/B4**
East 100th Street **155/F4-156/B4**
East 101st Street **155/F4-156/B4**
East 102nd Street **155/F4-156/B4**
East 103rd Street **155/F4-156/B4**
East 104th Street **156/C4**
East 105th Street **156/C4**
East 106th Street **156/C3**
East 107th Street **156/C3**
East 108th Street **156/C3**
East 109th Street **156/C3**
East 110th Street **156/C3**
East 111th Street **156/C2**
East 112th Street **156/C2**
East 113th Street **157/D3**
East 114th Street **157/E3**
East 115th Street **156/C2**
East 116th Street **156/C2**
East 117th Street **156/C2**
East 118th Street **156/C1**
East 119th Street **156/C1**
East 120th Street **157/D1**
East 121st Street **157/D1**
East 122nd Street **157/D1**
East 123rd Street **157/D1**
East 124th Street **157/D1**
East 125th Street (M. Luther King Jr. Blvd) **157/D1**
East Broadway **143/D3-E3**
East Drive **151/F3-152/A3**
East End Avenue **153/E2**
East Houston Street **143/D1**
East Road **153/D5-D6**
Eckford Street **149/E5**
Eighth Avenue **146/B4-147/D1-154/C6**
Eldridge Street **143/E3**
Elevated Highway **142/C6**
Eleventh Avenue **146/B3-B1**
Elizabeth Street **143/D3**
Engert Avenue **145/F2**
Entrance Street **148/A2**
Ericsson Place **142/B2**
Essex Street **143/E3**
Evans Street **144/A6**
Everitt Street **143/D6**
Exchange Place **142/B5**
Exit Street **148/A2**

F

Father Demo Square **146/C5**
Fifth Avenue **147/F1-D5-151/F4-152/A4-155/F4-156/C2-B4**
Filimore Place **145/D3**
Finn Square **142/B2**
First Avenue **143/E1-147/E6-148/A3-152/C5-156/C6-157/E3**
Flatbush Avenue **139/F2-140/A4**
Fletcher Street **142/C5**
Flushing Avenue **141/D1-145/F6**

Foley Square **142/C3**
Forsyth Street **143/E3**
Fourth Avenue **147/E5**
Frankfort Street **142/C4**
Franklin Avenue **141/D1-D3**
Franklin D. Roosevelt Drive (East River Drive) **144/B3-153/D4**
Franklin Street (Brooklyn) **149/D4**
Franklin Street (Manhattan) **142/C2-B2**
Frawley Circle **156/C2**
Frederick Douglass Boulevard **155/F2-156/B2**
Frederick Douglass Circle **155/E2-156/A2**
Freeman Street **148/C5**
Front Street (Brooklyn) **143/F6-E6**
Front Street (Manhattan) **142/C5**
Frost Street **145/E3**
Fulton Street (Brooklyn) **140/A3-141/E5**
Fulton Street (Manhattan) **142/B4**
Furman Street **139/D1-143/D6**

G

Gansevoort Street **146/B4**
Gem Street **145/E1**
G. Hartman Square **143/F2-144/A2**
Gold Street (Brooklyn) **139/F1-140/A1**
Gold Street (Manhattan) **142/C4**
Gouverneur Street **143/F3**
Gowanus Expressway **138/C6**
Graham Avenue **145/F1-F2**
Gramercy Park West **147/E4**
Grand Avenue **140/C1-141/D6-144/C3-145/E4**
Grand Street **142/C1**
Great Jones Street **147/D6**
Greene Street **143/D1-146/C6-147/D5**
Greenpoint Avenue **149/F5-D6**
Green Street **148/C5**
Greenwich Avenue **146/C4**
Greenwich Street **142/B3-146/B6**
Grove Street **146/B5**
Guernsey Street **149/D6**

H

Hanover Street (3) **142/B5**
Harrison Avenue **145/E5**
Harrison Street **142/B2**
Havemeyer Street **145/D5-D4**
Henry Hudson Parkway **154/A6**
Henry Street (Brooklyn) **139/E1-143/E6**
Henry Street (Manhattan) **143/D4-E3**
Hester Street **143/D2**
Hewes Street **145/E5-D6**
Heyward Street **141/D1-145/D6**
Hooper Street **145/E5-D6**
Hope Street **145/D3**
Hopkins Street **141/F1**
Horatio Street **146/B4**
Howard Street **142/C2**
Hubert Street **142/B2**
Hudson Avenue **144/A6**
Hudson Street **142/B1-146/B6**
Hugh L. Carey Tunnel **138/B3**

Humboldt Street **149/F5**
Huron Street **148/C5**

I

India Street **148/C5**
Irving Place **147/E5**

J

Jackson Avenue **149/D3**
Jackson Street **144/A3**
Jane Street **146/B4**
Java Street **148/C5**
Jay Street (Brooklyn) **143/F6**
Jay Street (Manhattan) **142/B2**
Jewel Street **149/E5**
Joe Dimaggio Highway (West Side Highway) **142/A5**
John Street (Brooklyn) **143/E5**
John Street (Manhattan) **142/B4**
Jones Street **146/C5**
Juliana Place **144/C5**

K

Keap Street **145/E5**
Kenmare Street **143/D2**
Kent Avenue **141/D1-144/C4-C5**
Kent Street **148/C5**
Kingsland Avenue **149/F4**
King Street **146/B6**

L

Lafayette Avenue **140/A4-145/E3**
Lafayette Street **142/C3-143/D2**
La Guardia Place **146/C6**
Laight Street **142/B2**
Lee Avenue **145/D5**
Lenox Avenue (Malcolm X Boulevard) **156/B2**
Leonard Street **142/B2**
Leroy Street **146/B5**
Levis Street **143/A3**
Lexington Avenue **147/E3-152/B4-156/C4-157/D2**
Liberty Street **142/A4**
Lincoln Place **140/C6-A5**
Lispenard Street **142/C2**
Little Street **144/A6**
Little West 12th Street **146/B3**
Long Island Expressway **149/E3**
Lorimer Street **141/E1-145/E2-149/D6**
Ludlow Street **143/E3**
Lynch Street **141/E1-145/E6**

M

Mac Dougal Street **146/C6**
Madison Avenue **147/E3-151/F4-152/B4-155/F4-156/C2-B4**
Madison Street **142/C4-143/E4**
Maiden Lane **142/B5**
Main Street (Brooklyn) **143/E6**
Main Street (Manhattan) **153/E4**
Manhattan Avenue (Brooklyn) **145/F2-F4**
Manhattan Avenue (Queens) **149/D4**
Manhattan Bridge **143/E4**
Marcy Avenue **145/D4-D5**
Market Street (Brooklyn) **140/B1-144/B6**
Market Street (Manhattan) **143/D3**

Marshall Street **143/F5-144/A5**
Martin-Luther-King Place **141/F1**
Maujer Street **145/E4**
McGuinness Boulevard **149/E4-E5**
Meeker Avenue **145/E3**
Mercer Street **142/C2-143/D1-147/D6**
Meserole Avenue **145/D1**
Metropolitan Avenue **144/C2-145/F3**
Middagg Street **143/D6**
Middleton Street **145/E6**
Milton Street **148/C6**
Monitor Street **149/F5**
Monroe Street **143/D4**
Montgomery Street **143/F3**
Montrose Avenue **145/F5**
Morningside Avenue **155/E2-156/A2**
Morris Street **142/A5**
Morton Street (Brooklyn) **144/C5**
Morton Street (Manhattan) **146/B5**
Mott Street **143/D3**
Moultrie Street **149/E5**
Mulberry Street **143/D3**
Murray Street **142/B3-A3**
Myrtle Avenue **139/F2-140/A2-C2-141/E2**

N

Nassau Avenue **145/F1-E2**
Nassau Street (Brooklyn) **139/F1**
Nassau Street (Manhattan) **142/B5**
Navy Street **140/A1-144/A6**
Newel Street **149/E5**
New Street **142/B5**
Ninth Avenue **146/B3-150/C6**
Noble Street **148/C6**
Norfolk Street **143/E3**
Norman Avenue **145/E1-149/E6**
North 1st Street **144/C3**
North 3rd Street **144/C2**
North 4th Street **145/D2**
North 5th Street **144/C2**
North 6th Street **145/D2**
North 7th Street **145/D2**
North 8th Street **145/D2-E2**
North 10th Street **145/D1**
North 11th Street **145/D1**
North 12th Street **145/D1**
North 13th Street **145/D1**
North 14th Street **145/D1**
North 15th Street **145/D1**
North End Avenue **142/A3**
North Henry Street **149/F5**
North Moore Street **142/B2**
Nostrand Avenue **141/F6-E1**

O

Oak Street **148/C6**
Old Slip **142/B5**
Oliver Street **143/D3**
One Police Plaza **142/C4**
Orange Street **139/D1-143/D6**
Orchard Street **143/E3**

P

Pacific Street **139/D3-E3-140/B5-145/E5**
Paidge Avenue **149/E4**

Paladino Avenue **157/E2**
Park Avenue (Brooklyn) **141/D2**
Park Avenue (Manhattan) **152/B4-156/C4-157/D2**
Park Avenue South **147/E4**
Park Row **142/C4**
Park Street **142/B3**
Pearl Street (Brooklyn) **139/F1-143/F6**
Pearl Street (Manhattan) **142/C3-C4-B5-A6**
Pearson Place **149/F3**
Pearson Street **149/F2**
Pell Street **143/D3**
Penn Street **145/D6**
Perleman Place **147/F5**
Perry Street **146/B5**
Pike Street **143/E3**
Pine Street **142/B5**
Pitt Street **143/F3**
Plymouth Street **143/F5**
Populer Street **143/E6**
Powers Street **145/E4**
President Street **138/C4-139/F5-D5**
Prince Street **146/C6**
Prospect Street **139/E1-143/E6**
Provost Street **149/E4**
Pulaski Bridge **149/E4**
Purves Street **149/F2**

Q

Quai Street **145/D1-148/C6**
Queensboro Bridge **153/D5**
Queens Midtown Tunnel **148/B2**

R

Reade Street **142/B3**
Rector Street **142/A4**
Renwick Street **142/B1**
Richardson Street **145/E2**
Ridge Street **143/F3**
Riverside Drive **154/C3-A6**
River Terrace **142/A3**
Rivington Street **143/E2**
Rodney Street **144/C6-145/D5-E5**
Roebling Street **145/D4-D5**
Ross Street **145/D5**
Russel Street **149/F5**
Rutgers Street **143/E3**
Rutherford Place **147/E5**
Rutledge Street **141/D1-145/D6**

S

Saint James Place **143/D4**
Saint Johns Lane **142/C2**
Saint Marks Place **147/E6**
Saint Nicholas Avenue **155/F1-156/B1**
Sands Street **139/F1-140/A1-143/F6-144/A6**
Second Avenue **143/E1-147/F4-E6-148/A3-152/C5-157/E2-D4**
Seventh Avenue **146/C4-B6-147/E1-151/D6**
Sheriff Street **144/A2**
Skillman Avenue **149/F3**
South 1st Street **144/C3-145/E4**
South 3rd Street **144/C3-145/E4**
South 4th Street **144/C4-145/E4**
South 5th Street **144/C4-145/D4**
South 6th Street **144/C4**

South 8th Street **144/C4**
South 9th Street **144/C4**
South 10th Street **144/C5**
South 11th Street **144/C5**
South End Avenue **142/A5**
South Street **142/B6-143/D4-E4**
Spring Street **142/C1-B1-146/B6**
Spruce Street **142/C4**
Staple Street **142/B3**
State Street **142/B6**
Station Street **143/E1**
Steuben Street **140/C1**
Stone Street **142/B5**
Suffolk Street **143/C1**
Sutton Street **149/F6**

T

Taylor Street **144/C6-C5**
Ten Eyck Street **145/E4**
Tenth Avenue **146/B3**
Third Avenue **147/E5-148/A2-152/B5-156/B6-157/D2**
Thomas Street **142/B3**
Thompson Street **142/C2**
Thomson Avenue **149/F2**
Throop Avenue **145/F5**
Tiffany Place **138/C4**
Tillary Street **139/E2**
Transverse Road No 1 **151/E2-152/A2**
Transverse Road No 2 **155/D6**
Transverse Road No 3 **155/D5**
Transverse Road No 4 **155/E4-156/A4**
Triborough Bridge **157/F2-F4-F5**
Trimble Place **142/C3**
Trinity Place **142/A5**

U

Union Avenue **145/E2-E4**
University Place **147/D5**

V

Van Brunt Street **138/C4**
Vandam Street **142/C1-146/B6**
Vanderbilt Avenue **140/C6-B1**
Varick Street **142/C2**
Vernon Boulevard **149/D3-153/E6**
Vesey Street **142/A3-B3**
Vestry Street **142/B1**
Vietnam Veterans Memorial Plaza **142/B6**

W

Wagner Place **142/C4**
Walker Street **142/C2**
Wallabout Street **141/D1-145/F6**
Wall Street **142/B5**
Walton Street **141/E1-145/E6**
Warren Street **142/A3**
Washington Avenue **140/C5-C1**
Washington Place **146/C5-147/D5**
Washington Square East **147/D6**
Washington Square North **146/C5**
Washington Square South **146/C5**
Washington Square West **146/C5**
Washington Street (Brooklyn) **143/E6**
Washington Street (Manhattan) **142/A5-B2-146/B4**
Water Street (Brooklyn) **143/F6-E6**

Water Street (Manhattan) **142/B6-C5-143/F4-D4**
Watts Street **142/B1**
Waverly Place **146/C5-C4-147/D5**
West 3rd Street **146/C5**
West 4th Street **146/C5-C4-147/D6**
West 8th Street **146/C5**
West 9th Street **146/C5**
West 10th Street **146/B5**
West 11th Street **146/C4-B4**
West 12th Street **146/C4-B4**
West 13th Street **146/B3**
West 14th Street **146/B3**
West 15th Street **146/B3**
West 16th Street **146/B3**
West 17th Street **146/B3**
West 18th Street **146/B2**
West 19th Street **146/B2**
West 20th Street **146/B2**
West 21st Street **146/B2**
West 22nd Street **146/C2**
West 23rd Street **146/B2**
West 24th Street **146/B1**
West 25th Street **146/B1**
West 26th Street **146/B1**
West 27th Street **146/B1-150/A6**
West 28th Street **146/B1-150/A6**
West 29th Street **150/A6**
West 30th Street **150/A6**
West 31st Street **146/C1-150/B6**
West 32nd Street **147/D1-150/B6**
West 33rd Street **150/A6**
West 34th Street **150/A5**
West 35th Street **150/B6**
West 36th Street **150/B5**
West 37th Street **150/B5**
West 38th Street **150/B5**
West 39th Street **150/B5**
West 40th Street **150/B5**
West 41st Street **150/B4**
West 42nd Street **150/B4**
West 43rd Street **150/B4**
West 44th Street **150/B4**
West 45th Street **150/B4**
West 46th Street **150/B4**
West 47th Street (Diamond Row) **150/B4**
West 48th Street **150/B4**
West 49th Street **150/B3**
West 50th Street **150/B3**
West 51st Street **150/C3**
West 52nd Street **150/C3**
West 53rd Street **150/C3**
West 54th Street **150/C3**
West 55th Street **150/C3**
West 56th Street **150/C3**
West 57th Street **150/C3**
West 58th Street **150/C2-151/E3**
West 59th Street **150/C2**
West 60th Street **150/C2**
West 61st Street **150/C2**
West 62nd Street **151/D2**
West 63rd Street **151/E2**
West 64th Street **151/D2**
West 65th Street **151/D2**
West 66th Street **151/D1**
West 67th Street **151/D1**
West 68th Street **151/E1**
West 69th Street **151/E1**
West 70th Street **151/D1**
West 71st Street **154/A6**

West 72nd Street **151/D1-154/A6**
West 73rd Street **154/A6**
West 74th Street **154/A6**
West 75th Street **154/A6**
West 76th Street **154/B5**
West 77th Street **154/B5**
West 78th Street **154/B5**
West 79th Street **154/B5**
West 80th Street **154/B5**
West 81st Street **154/B5**
West 82nd Street **154/B5**
West 83rd Street **154/B5**
West 84th Street (Edgar Allen Poe Street) **154/B4**
West 85th Street **154/B4**
West 86th Street **154/B4**
West 87th Street **154/B4**
West 88th Street **154/B4**
West 89th Street **154/B4**
West 90th Street (Henry J. Browne Boulevard) **154/C4**
West 91st Street **154/C3**
West 92nd Street **154/C3**
West 93rd Street **154/C3**
West 94th Street **154/C3**
West 95th Street **154/C3**
West 96th Street **154/C3**
West 97th Street **154/C3**
West 98th Street **154/C2**
West 99th Street **154/C2**
West 100th Street **154/C2**
West 101st Street **154/C2-155/E3-156/A3**
West 102nd Street **154/C2**
West 103rd Street **155/D2-156/A3**
West 104th Street **155/D2**
West 105th Street **155/D2**
West 106th Street **155/D1**
West 107th Street **155/D1**
West 108th Street **155/D1**
West 109th Street **155/D1**
West 111th Street **155/D1-156/A2**
West 112th Street **155/E1-156/A1**
West 113th Street **155/F1-156/B1**
West 115th Street **155/F1-156/A1**
West 116th Street **155/F1-156/A1**
West Broadway **142/C2-B4**
West Drive **151/E3-152/A1-155/E4-156/A4**
West End Avenue **150/C2-154/C3**
West Houston Street **146/C6-B6**
West Road **153/E4-D5-D6**
West Street **144/A6-148/C4**
West Thames Street **142/A4**
Whitehall Street **142/B5**
White Street **142/C2**
Willett Street **143/F3-144/A3**
Williamsburg Bridge **144/B3**
William Street **142/B5**
Wilson Street **144/C5**
Wooster Street **142/C2**
Worth Street **142/B3**
Wythe Avenue **141/D1-144/C4-145/D6**
Wythe Place **144/C5**

Y

York Avenue **153/D4**
York Street (Brooklyn) **143/F6**
York Street (Manhattan) **142/C2**

Motorway Autobahn		Autoroute Autosnelweg
Highway with four lanes Vierspurige Straße		Route à quatre voies Weg met vier rijstroken
Through highway Durchgangsstraße		Route de transit Weg voor doorgaand verkeer
Main road Hauptstraße		Route principale Hoofdweg
Other roads Sonstige Straßen		Autres routes Overige wegen
Main railway - Other railway Hauptbahn - Sonstige Bahn		Chemin de fer principal - Autre ligne Belangrijke spoorweg - Overige spoorweg
Ferry Fähre		Bac Veer
Subway U-Bahn	•••M•••	Métro Ondergrondse spoorweg
Express station Expressstation	•••M•••	Station exprès Expresstation
One-way street Einbahnstraße		Rue à sens unique Straat met eenrichtingsverkeer
Information Information	🛈	Information Informatie
Police station - Post office Polizeistation - Postamt	● ✆	Poste de police - Bureau de poste Politiebureau - Postkantoor
Monument - Synagogue Denkmal - Synagoge	♟ ✡	Monument - Synagogue Monument - Synagoge
Church of interest - Other church Sehenswerte Kirche - Sonstige Kirche	✚ ✚	Église remarquable - Autre église Bezienswaardige kerk - Andere kerk
Hospital Krankenhaus	Ⓗ	Hôpital Ziekenhuis
Lighthouse - Heliport Leuchtturm - Hubschrauberlandeplatz	⟟ ⊙	Phare - Héliport Vuurtoren - Heliport
Pedestrian zone Fußgängerzone		Zone piétonne Voetgangerszone
Built-up area, public building Bebaute Fläche, öffentliches Gebäude		Zone bâtie, bâtiment public Bebouwing, openbaar gebouw
Housing project Wohnkomplex		Pâté résidentiel Huizencomplex
Building of interest Sehenswertes Gebäude		Bâtiment remarquable Bezienswaardig gebouw
Park - Industrial area Park - Industriegelände		Parc - Zone industrielle Park - Industrieterrein
MARCO POLO Discovery Tour 1 MARCO POLO Erlebnistour 1		MARCO POLO Tour d'aventure 1 MARCO POLO Avontuurlijke Route 1
MARCO POLO Discovery Tours MARCO POLO Erlebnistouren		MARCO POLO Tours d'aventure MARCO POLO Avontuurlijke Routes
MARCO POLO Highlight	⭐①	MARCO POLO Highlight

FOR YOUR NEXT TRIP...

MARCO POLO TRAVEL GUIDES

Algarve
Amsterdam
Andalucia
Athens
Australia
Austria
Bali & Lombok
Bangkok
Barcelona
Berlin
Brazil
Bruges
Brussels
Budapest
Bulgaria
California
Cambodia
Canada East
Canada West / Rockies
& Vancouver
Cape Town &
Garden Route
Cape Verde
Channel Islands
Chicago & The Lakes
China
Cologne
Copenhagen
Corfu
Costa Blanca
& Valencia
Costa Brava
Costa del Sol & Granada
Crete
Cuba
Cyprus (North and
South)
Devon & Cornwall
Dresden
Dubai

Dublin
Dubrovnik &
Dalmatian Coast
Edinburgh
Egypt
Egypt Red Sea Resorts
Finland
Florence
Florida
French Atlantic Coast
French Riviera
(Nice, Cannes & Monaco)
Fuerteventura
Gran Canaria
Greece
Hamburg
Hong Kong & Macau
Iceland
India
India South
Ireland
Israel
Istanbul
Italy
Japan
Jordan
Kos
Krakow
Lake Garda
Lanzarote
Las Vegas
Lisbon
London
Los Angeles
Madeira & Porto Santo
Madrid
Mallorca
Malta & Gozo
Mauritius
Menorca

Milan
Montenegro
Morocco
Munich
Naples & Amalfi Coast
New York
New Zealand
Norway
Oslo
Oxford
Paris
Peru & Bolivia
Phuket
Portugal
Prague
Rhodes
Rome
Salzburg
San Francisco
Santorini
Sardinia
Scotland
Seychelles
Shanghai
Sicily
Singapore
South Africa
Sri Lanka
Stockholm
Switzerland
Tenerife
Thailand
Turkey
Turkey South Coast
Tuscany
United Arab Emirates
USA Southwest
(Las Vegas, Colorado,
New Mexico, Arizona
& Utah)
Venice
Vienna
Vietnam
Zakynthos & Ithaca,
Kefalonia, Lefkas

The travel guides with
Insider
Tips

INDEX

This index lists all sights and destinations, plus some of the most important streets, squares, quarters and people featured in this guide. Numbers in bold indicate a main entry.

101 Spring Street 111
432 Park Avenue 22
550 Madison Avenue **46**
9/11 Memorial **29**, 114
Amagansett 25
American Folk Art Museum 49
American Museum of Natural
    History **50**, 122
Avenue of the Americas 35
Barclays Center **93**
Battery Park **28**, 115
Battery Park City 29
Battery Place 115
Bedford Avenue 73
Beekman Tower 22
Bergdorf Goodman 38, **76**
Bleecker Street 111
Bloomingdale's **76**
Blue Note 91
BoCoCa 74
Bowery 37, 88, 113
Bridgehampton 25
Broadway 24, 26, **35**, 36, 48, 52,
    72, 88, 111, 114
Broadway musicals **24**, **88**, 131
Bronx 17, 58
Bronx Zoo **122**
Brookfield Place **29**
Brooklyn 15, 17, 18, 22, 23, 30, 51,
    55, 56, 57, 58, 70, 73, 87, 88, 93,
    95, 103, 104, 105, 119, 120, 121,
    131
Brooklyn Bridge 15, 22, **30**, 55, 110
Brooklyn Bridge Park 23, 55, 57, 120
Brooklyn Heights 55, 120
Brooklyn Museum **55**
Bryant Park **40**, 51
Bushwick 17, 24
Canal Street **36**, 110, 112
Carnegie Hall 93
Carroll Gardens **56**
Castle Clinton 115
Central Park 16, 20, 48, **50**, 67, 90,
    93, 117, 125
Central Park West 51, 125
Central Park Zoo 51
Chase Manhattan Plaza 116
Chelsea 22, 37, 70, 73, 75
Children's Museum of Art **122**
Children's Museum of
    Manhattan **122**
Chinatown 24, 32, **34**, 36, 79, 81,
    110, 112, 124
Christie's 45
Christopher Street **38**
Chrysler Building 21, 40, **41**
Circle Line 128
Citi Field Stadium 58
City Center 94
City Hall **31**, 114
City Island 23
Cloisters **56**
Columbus Circle 67
Comcast Building 45, 117
Coney Island 23, **56**
Cooper-Hewitt Museum **51**
Culinary Institute of America 59
Dakota Building 51, 117
David Geffen Hall **93**

David H. Koch Theater **94**
Dean & DeLuca **75**, 111
Downtown 22, 104
Duane Park 114
Dumbo 56, 61, 119
East Hampton 25
East Village 32, **37**, 67, 100, 110, 113
Ellis Island 23, **31**, 33, 115
Empire State Building 15, 21, 26,
    28, 38, **41**, 102, 108
Fifth Avenue 26, **38**, 46, 72, 84,
    107, 117, 124, 125
Fifth Avenue (Brooklyn) 104
Financial District 34
Fire Island 25
First Place 115
Flatiron Building 107
Fort Tryon Park 56
Fraunces Tavern 116
Frederick P. Rose Hall **53**
Frick Collection **52**, 117
General Post Office 133
George Washington Bridge 56
Governors Island 23, **57**
Grand Central Terminal 26, 40, **42**,
    66, 109
Grand Street 113
Greene Street 36
Greenpoint 24, **57**, 87
Greenwich Village 24, **37**, 38, 82,
    92, 110
Ground Zero **29**
Guggenheim Museum 38, 49, **52**, 118
Hamptons 25
Harlem 17, 20, 36, **52**, 71, 92, 95,
    103
Hell's Kitchen 101
Herald Square 72
High Line Park 22, 99, 110
Houston Street 72
Hudson River Park 15, 22, 51, 123
Hudson River Valley **59**
Hyde Park 59
International Center of
    Photography **36**
John F. Kennedy Airport 128
La Guardia Airport 128
Lever House 22
Liberty Island 23
Lincoln Center 47, 49, **52**, 125
Little Italy 24, **34**, 36, 73, 111, 112
Long Island 25
Lower East Side 24, **37**, 66, 68, 73,
    82, 89, 97, 98, 101, 113
Lower Manhattan 28
LuSTO 73
Macy's 72, **76**, 125
Madison Avenue **43**, 72, 117, 117
Madison Square Garden 58
Madison Square Park 108
Manhattan 14, 17, 18, 22, 23, 25,
    27, 28, 29, 30, 31, 32, 34, 36, 38,
    45, 51, 54, 55, 58, 73, 93, 102,
    103, 105, 114, 128, 168
Manhattan Bridge 36
McCarren Park 57
Meatpacking District 40, 73, 84, 89,
    98, 100
Metlife Stadium 58

Metropolitan Museum of Art 38,
    49, **53**, 56, 117
Metropolitan Opera 48, 52, 93,
    94, 124
Midtown 36, **40**, 72, 84, 85, 128
Montauk 25
Municipal Building 31, 114
Museum of Art and Design 67
Museum of Jewish Heritage **31**, 116
Museum of Modern Art 28, **43**, 81,
    109, 125
Museum of Sex **44**
Museum of the Moving Image **57**
Musicals **24**, **88**, 131
National Museum of the American
    Indian **32**, 116
NBC 45
Neue Galerie New York **54**, 118
New Jersey 128
New Museum of
    Contemporary Art 14, **36**
New York Aquarium 56, **123**
New York Historical Society **54**
New York Public Library **44**
New York State Parks **18**
New York University (NYU) 111
Newark 128
NoLita **55**
Old Merchant's House 38
One World Trade Center 13, 22, 28,
    32, 115, 127
One57 22
Orchard Street 113
P. S. 1 Contemporary Art Center **58**
Park Avenue 109
Park Slope 56, 73
Prospect Park 17, 51, 93
Public Libraries 131
Queens 17, 23, 51, 58, 100, 105, 128
Radio City Music Hall **45**
Randall's Island 23
Red Hook **58**
Rhinebeck 59
Rockefeller Center 38, **45**, 51, 101,
    117, 125, 127
Rockefeller Center Museum 45
Rockefeller Estate 59
Roosevelt Island 23, 123
Roosevelt Island Tramway **123**
Rubin Museum of Art **39**
Seagram Building 22
Sixth Avenue 35, 125
Skyscraper Museum **32**, 116
SoHo **34**, 35, 36, 73, 78, 87, 97, 111
Sony Building
    (505 Madison Avenue) **46**
South Hampton 25
South Street Seaport 116
St John the Divine 55
St Marks Place **40**, 113
St Patrick's Cathedral **46**
St Paul's Chapel **32**, 114
Staten Island 17, 23, 28
Staten Island Ferry **33**
Statue of Liberty 17, 23, 28, **33**, 109,
    114, 115, 129
Stock Exchange **33**
Strawberry Fields 117
Tenement Museum 38, **40**

Theater District 40, **46**, 82, 88
Tiffany & Co. 38, **79**, 117
Time Warner Center **47**, 53
Times Square 15, 22, 26, 46, 99, 101, 108
Tompkins Square Park 113
Top of the Rock 45
TriBeCa 22, 28, **33**, 36, 48, 98, 124
Trinity Church 115

Trump Tower **47**
United Nations 15, **47**, 68
Upper East Side 22, **48**, 49, 72
Upper West Side 22, 36, **48**, 101
Uptown 22, **48**
Verrazano Bridge 125
Waldorf-Astoria **48**
Wall Street 28, **34**, 115, 116
Washington Square 38, **40**, 103, 111

Washington, George 32, 40
West Village 22, 36
Whitney Museum of American Art **40**
Williamsburg 17, 24, 57, **58**, 66, 79, 90, 103
Woolworth Building 114
World Trade Center 21, 28, 29, 32, 124
Yankee Stadium 58

WRITE TO US

e@mail: info@marcopologuides.co.uk
Did you have a great holiday? Is there something on your mind? Whatever it is, let us know! Whether you want to praise, alert us to errors or give us a personal tip – MARCO POLO would be pleased to hear from you.
We do everything we can to provide the very latest information for your trip. Nevertheless, despite all of our authors'

thorough research, errors can creep in. MARCO POLO does not accept any liability for this. Please contact us by e@mail or post.

MARCO POLO Travel Publishing Ltd
Pinewood, Chineham Business Park
Crockford Lane, Chineham
Basingstoke, Hampshire RG24 8AL
United Kingdom

CREDITS

Cover photograph: Manhattan (Schapowalow: O. Fantuz)
Photos: DuMont Bildarchiv: Sasse (9, 122/123); huber-images: S. Amantini (59), A. Bartuccio (109), M. Borchi (23, 41), L. Caccarella (53), P. Canali (14/15, 26/27), F. Carovillano (18 center, 46/47, 74), C. Cassaro (4 top, 94, 140/141), C. Claudio (113), O. Fantuz (34, 43), S. Kremer (2, 4 bottom, 12/13, 38, 45, 106/107, 110), M. Rellini (6, 11, 17, 20/21, 50, 54, 57, 78, 87, 120), A. Serrano (flap top), R. Spila (flap bottom), R. Taylor (25, 31, 56), S. Torrione (91, 101); © iStockphoto: Jon Faulknor (18 bottom); Laif: Falke (124/125), Gebhard (127), Heeb (10, 82/83, 105), Jonkmanns (126 top), Kurz (122), Linkel (72/73), Sasse (5, 33, 68 l., 92, 123, 126 bottom); Laif/Redux (60/61); Laif/UPI: Graff (124); mauritius images/age (8, 125); mauritius images/age fotostock: R. Levine (77); mauritius images/Alamy (7, 37, 55, 62, 65, 66/67, 84), R. Duchaine (71), R. Levine (80); mauritius images/CuboImages (98); mauritius images/FreshFood (68 r.); mauritius images/Mint Images Ltd. (3); Schapowalow: S. Amantini (102), O. Fantuz (1); Schapowalow/4Corners: J. Foulkes (19 bottom); Schapowalow/SIME: P. Canali (48, 96/97), C. Cassaro (19 top), M. Relini (88/89), M. Rellini (133); Sycamore: Ole Sondresen (18 top)

4th Edition 2018 – fully revised and updated
Worldwide Distribution: Marco Polo Travel Publishing Ltd, Pinewood, Chineham Business Park, Crockford Lane, Basingstoke, Hampshire RG24 8AL, United Kingdom. Email: sales@marcopolouk.com
© MAIRDUMONT GmbH & Co. KG, Ostfildern
Chief editor: Marion Zorn
Author: Doris Chevron; co-author: Alrun Steinrueck; editor: Jens Bey
Programme supervision: Susanne Heimburger, Nikolai Michaelis, Martin Silbermann, Kristin Wittemann
Picture editor: Gabriele Forst
What's hot: Alrun Steinrueck, wunder media, Munich
Cartography street atlas: © MAIRDUMONT, Ostfildern; Cartography pull-out map: © MAIRDUMONT, Ostfildern
Front cover, pull-out map cover, page 1: Karl Anders – Büro für Visual Stories, Hamburg; design: milchhof : atelier, Berlin; design p. 2/3, Discovery Tours: Susan Chaaban Dipl.-Des. (FH)
Translated from German by Birgitt Lederer, Jennifer Walcoff Neuheiser; editor of the English edition: Margaret Howie, fullproof.co.za

DOS & DON'TS 👍

A few things you should bear in mind in New York

DON'T WALK IN THE PARK AFTER DARK

Today New York and especially Manhattan are no more risky than other big cities like London. However it makes sense not to carry a lot of cash in your wallet and keep it on your person discreetly. Don't wear any valuables in public and women should consider carrying their handbags across their chests. Best to ignore drug dealers completely, but you can give beggars a dollar bill! When a stranger tries to engage you in conversation it is often a diversion tactic and they usually have an accomplice working with them. Once it gets dark do not go for a walk in the park and avoid quiet, poorly lit streets.

DON'T FORGET YOUR PASSPORT

You have to show your passport for security reasons at some sightseeing spots. Many bars may also want to see an ID even though you are clearly over 21.

DO AVOID JET LAG

On arrival stay up for several hours before sleeping (you will usually arrive in the afternoon European time if your flight leaves from Europe). You will not notice the time difference as much after three days if you follow this simple rule.

The question you may well ask: what is there to do at 5am or 6am in the morning in New York? Visit the fish or meat market, listen to some jazz at *Small's*, have your first cup of coffee of the day at a corner shop or get into the American way of life by watching breakfast television.

DO AVOID CLAIMS TO FAME

Walls adorned with signed photos by celebs singing the praises of your nearest local or pizzeria are a common occurrence in New York. Also best to avoid the feeding frenzy at *Sardi's*, *Gallagher's Steak House* and any restaurants inundated by busloads of patrons. Steer clear of *Michael's Pub* a music bar where Woody Allen plays the clarinet on a Monday. In all honesty, you will have a better chance of bumping into him walking through Central Park on a Sunday morning.

DO TAKE THE RIGHT TAXI

At both the airport and outside hotels drivers without licenses will offer visitors their "taxi" services. They are seldom insured and charge exorbitant rates. The same applies when hailing down a non-yellow cab. Some New Yorkers will use these *gypsy cabs* but they know what they are letting themselves in for and how to negotiate the price.